Gerd Wolfgang

111 Places
in Venice
That You
Must Not Miss

111

emons:

© Emons Verlag GmbH
All rights reserved
© Photographs: Gerd Wolfgang Sievers
Design: Eva Kraskes, based on a design
by Lübbeke | Naumann | Thoben
Maps: altancicek.design, www.altancicek.de
English translation: Kathleen Becker
Printing and binding: Grafisches Centrum Cuno, Calbe
Printed in Germany 2014
ISBN 978-3-95451-460-1
First edition

Did you enjoy it? Do you want more?
Join us in uncovering new places around the world on:
www.111places.com

Foreword

"Everything that can be said and written about Venice has been said and written!" The author of these words was Johann Wolfgang von Goethe in 1786, no less. Yet what hasn't since been said, written and printed about the Serenissima? Paper is patient, as is Venice actually, most of the time anyway.

The book you're holding in your hands now, *111 Places in Venice*, might not surprise you in its every choice; some things you'll probably be familiar with, at least by name. Yet there are stories associated with these places that are not often told and are mostly unknown to Venetians today. Venice is imbued with a particular characteristic that you could perhaps describe as "Truth is Perception", and visitors may first have to learn to deal with this "dietrologia" – a search for hidden meanings, if you will.

Venice not only has a penchant for the finer things in life, which you'll encounter in the shape of permissive (mostly female) saints, a variety of "cicchetti" (delicious snacks), quaffable wine and effervescent refreshing spritz, but the city also has a love for obscure, opaque and adventurous stories. These may have a religious, esoteric, alchemistic, pecuniary or (rarely) political or military origin, or indeed be inspired by lust, sexual indiscretions or frenzied gatherings. Nothing seems to be, or has been, unheard of previously. The Serenissima – the New York of bygone days?

This book tells the lesser-known stories of Venice, leading you to places you'll enjoy spending time, maybe in the company of friends, discussing life, eating and drinking, or simply on your own. Since times immemorial, Venice has been a singular pleasure, and I remain convinced that Venice will always remain Venice. What's that old ditty: *there's life in the old dog yet!*

111 Places

1 Essi Buranei & Co
Pastries and doughnuts

Old Venice has a strong tradition of pastry making, and the list of sweets, biscuits, cakes and doughnuts, created here over the course of centuries is nearly endless. Every occasion has its dedicated delicacies. While the most extravagant sweet sins were born from the tradition of the Venetian carnival, some "dolci" owe their existence to other cuisines.

Let's start with the "baicoli", a kind of sweet double-baked biscuit, that's quite labour intensive to make, and today is still sold everywhere in tin cans. Many pastry shop display windows are adorned with "dolce di albumi", meringue-style sweets in various colours, and "biscotti alla veneziana", biscotti flavoured with vanilla and amaretto, that are best enjoyed with a sweet wine.

"The Venetians' worst vice is gluttony!" as the city historian, Pietro Gasparo Morolin, lamented in 1841, most probably referring to the doughnuts indispensable at Carnival, such as "fritole" (with raisins), "frittelle di zucca" (with pumpkin), "frittelle veneziane" (Venetian doughnuts with candied lemon peel and pine kernels) and the sweet alla Amaretti almond biscuits, "zaleti" (cornflour biscuits flavoured with grappa and raisins) or "bussolai buranelli", the sweet doughnuts from Burano, which are baked with a large quantity of eggs and a dash of rum.

The venerable Panificio Garbo on Burano, its seductive bakery scent seemingly enticing half the island, is famous for their "essi buranei", a biscuit in the shape of an S, similar to biscotti, and particularly appreciated as an accompaniment to zabaglione. The zabaglione is beaten by hand in a copper pot the traditional way, while you watch at your table at Ristorante da Poggi (see page 46). You will understand why Casanova loved this sweet as foreplay, rather than as a dessert.

Address Pasticceria Garbo, Via S. Mauro, Burano 336, 30142 Venice, tel. 0039/41735289 | Opening times In the summer months usually open daily; in the winter irregular opening hours | Vaporetto fermata Burano, line 9, 12, 14, night route N | Tip Venice also boasts a number of excellent pasticcerie, such as Tonolo (Dorsoduro 3764), Rizziardini (S. Polo, 1415 Campiello dei Meloni) or Rio Marin (Santa Croce 784).

2__Merletto

Lace and the anti-luxury laws

The "Dalla Lidia Merletti d'Arte" boutique, known for the finest bedspreads, lacy handkerchiefs, table runners, party finery and veils, as well as sensual and erotic lingerie made from lace, can't really be called an insider tip. However, few people know why it is lace that became the great artisanal craft of Venice, culminating in the "Punto in aria", a kind of freehand embroidery that doesn't use aids such as bobbins or crochet needles. This particular custom only occurs on Burano. And that, has a great deal to do with the city's history; both with regards to lingerie, an elementary accoutrement for erotic pleasures, and the laws of the time.

For centuries, visitors to Venice have commented on the extravagance of the Serenissima. However, deep down, the Venetians are merchants, usually tempering their love of consumption with an opposition to senseless waste. And as the Venetian love of money was only matched by their desire to create laws, 1299 saw the enactment of anti-luxury laws that were amended – tightened, really – again and again. A law from 1511, for instance, limited the amount that could be spent on jewellery to 50 ducats for a single string of pearls, and forbade the neckline to be adorned in any additional way.

At one time, when jewellery was prohibited entirely, the ladies of Venice started to wear beautifully embroidered lace scarves that covered their ears, and this lace was soon worth more than any jewellery. The subsequent ban on brocade rang in the era of precious lace lingerie, with its sensually cut slits, which made men even wilder than before. Viewed from this angle, these laws may not seem as silly as at first glance. Or was this all the result of careful planning in a man's world, a way to finally bring erotic lingerie into the marketplace?

Address Dalla Lidia Merletti d'Arte, Via Galuppi, Burano 215, 30142 Burano, tel. 0039/
41730052, www.dallalidia.com | Opening times Daily 9.30am–6.30pm (however, to avoid
being trampled underfoot by huge contingents of tourists it's inadvisable to arrive on a Friday
or Saturday.) | Vaporetto fermata Burano, line 9, 12, 14, night route N | Tip As brocade
is no longer forbidden – thank goodness – you may visit the famous Tessitura Luigi
Bevilacqua for some shopping or (by appointment) to simply admire the old looms
(www.luigi-bevilacqua.com).

3__ Venissa

Vineyard with a bell tower

Mazzorbo is a paradise and a wonderful place of refuge for those seeking a rest from the hectic hustle and bustle of Venice, yet also looking to enjoy food in stylish surroundings.

In the shadow of a venerable campanile jutting out from beyond a plain brick wall, the calm is as enticing as the summery scents of roses, lavender and meadow herbs. The whole scenario is dominated, though, by an old vineyard, known by the fine name of Scarpa-Volo.

Owned by the city of Venice, it was in danger of falling into disrepair. To avoid the complete ruin of this land, cultivated for centuries, its exploitation was put out to tender.

The best concept was apparently presented by the Bisol family from the eponymous Veneto vineyard, who are now growing fruits and vegetables organically. Accompanying studies are aiming to help maintain the fragile ecological balance in the lagoon, threatened in some locations.

In order to recoup at least part of the cost, a classy agritourist set-up has been created, which also offers overnight accommodations. Yet the icing on the cake is the upscale restaurant within the vineyard, including a terrace view of the campanile. The cuisine is made from ingredients sourced from their own farm, as well as from traditional products from the lagoon. This world-class restaurant, which only serves a maximum of 20 guests, has also been awarded a Michelin star.

At Venissa's you may sample the wine from the vineyard, for a fee, as the vineyard is small and the fine wine a rarity. To visually emphasize the value of the liquid gems, Venissa's small wine bottles are made from Murano glass, inscribed by hand, and labeled with real gold leaf – enough said!

Address Venissa, Fondamenta Santa Caterina, Isola di Mazzorbo 3, 30170 Venice, www.venissa.it | Opening times Wed – Mon, lunch: 12 noon – 2.30pm; dinner: 7 – 9.20pm | Vaporetto fermata Mazzorbo, line 12, night route N | Tip Not far from Venissa, the Trattoria Maddalena is a sound culinary option. If you have time on your hands, wander straight across the vineyard and step through the gate at the other end, which leads to a wooden bridge, that takes walkers directly to Burano.

4__Lucio Bubacco

Glass extravaganza

Murano is world-famous for its mouth-blown glass, and many people believe – wrongly – that the artisans producing these delicate miniatures are mainly there to please tourists. In fact, there are master craftsmen amongst them. One of the most distinguished artists is Lucio Bubacco; nobody makes the stiff glass come alive the way he does. The material seems to melt in his hands, only to reemerge in new and highly erotic shapes, like a phoenix rising from the ashes to please the world with explicit sexual representations. Watching him work is like witnessing magic.

Bubacco was born on the island of Murano (where he still lives) and has been working with glass since he was a child. He's spent a lifetime honing his craft and his magical creations can be found in museums and private collections the world over.

Bubacco's figures seem to form a seamless connection to the sins of bygone days and to revive the shamelessness of the old Serenissima. Whether his sculptures portray dancing ladies, copulating bodies, heterosexuals, transsexuals, lesbians, or gays – all preferences and proclivities are adequately represented in his menagerie.

With his creations, Bubacco is continuing a long tradition, as there are few other places where art is so closely connected with eroticism as it is in Venice. However, in contrast to Old Venice, which held a skeptical attitude towards homosexuality, Bubacco is particularly well known and appreciated within the gay community, as his devils are icons of masculinity; their representations don't leave much to the imagination.

And just as men today are free to love each other, women are also equally liberated and adventurous when it comes to the pleasures of the flesh. To loosely quote the Hungarian author Ludwig Hevesi: each era has its love; give love its freedom!

Address Fondamenta da Mula, Murano 148, 30141 Venice, tel. 0039/41736544, www.luciobubacco.com | **Opening times** The workshop may only be visited for exceptional reasons by prior appointment; info@luciobubacco.com | **Vaporetto fermata** Da Mula, line 3, 4.1/4.2 | **Tip** Across from Lucio Bubacco's workshop on the opposite side of the canal (simply cross the bridge and keep left), the Ristorante Ai Frati is considered one of the best fish restaurants in the lagoon (www.aifrati.com).

5__ Serenella

The lagoon, a legend … and more legends

While the UNESCO World Heritage site of the lagoon comprises over 600 square kilometres, only a fraction of this is inhabitable dry land.

In order to supply this island city, over 30 million tons of goods have to be transported by boat through the lagoon every year. The low water levels, at some points measuring only a few centimetres, represent the greatest danger for shipping here. The solution lies in a detail that the ancients were already trying to work out: keeping the prow depth as low as possible. The pioneers of this technology were the Romans, who constructed ships for transporting goods on rivers that were only several centimetres deep, yet were able to bear loads weighing over 35 tons.

The gondolas, as we know them today, are beloved from Las Vegas to Beijing, and by tourists – but no real Venetian would ever stray onto one of those one-man rowing boats. The type of boat that has been ruling the waters of the lagoon for centuries is called a "topi", which are smaller or medium-sized barges. Originally carved from wood, today the preferred material for this kind of boat is the lighter and more versatile fibreglass.

The undisputed queen of the lagoon is the serenella. "A tradition of quality and style" is the motto of these elegant boats, and every specimen – no more than four are produced each year – is one of a kind. A serenella withstands comparison to a Rolls-Royce; there is no market for used ones.

However, the shipyards could hardly survive without what they call new markets. Yet Venice needs its serenella. Any "taxi skipper" who wants to uphold a certain reputation drives one of these classy gleaming gems; a serenella tells – as does the skipper – legends of passion!

Address Cantiere Motonautico Serenella (yard), Sacca Serenella, Murano, 30141 Venice, tel. 0039/41739792 | **Opening times** They can't be visited as such, but you may ask for permission by emailing info@cantiereserenella.com | **Vaporetto fermata** Serenella, line 4.1/4.2, night route N | **Tip** In Venice people have a saying: "barca xe casa" (meaning: "we're at home on boats"). The non-profit association Arzanà has its headquarters in a 15th-century gondola yard and restores traditional boats. They run a small fleet of nearly 50 historic ships, amongst them a "peata" (freight ship) and a "gondolin da fresco", the last remaining refreshment gondola for trips into the lagoon. Visits by prior appointment; contact info@venetianboat.com (www.arzana.org).

6__The "Vitae"

... and Casanova's none-too-chaste nun

There is something futuristic and utopian about the "Vitae", a glass statue in Murano, designed by Denise Gemin. It radiates an odd mystique, a faceless aloofness, yet is still incredibly attractive; something born out of the imagination, but very real too – a blend of fiction and reality that becomes a charming whole.

The same charm of the unknown shrouds a certain nun, known only as M.M., who has kept generations of Casanovisti busy, with no one ever able to establish her true identity. We only know that she was a rather unchaste nun from one of the Murano convents, who was both Casanova's lover and the mistress of a high dignitary. What is documented, however, is the passion with which Casanova desired his nun, and that he slurped oysters with her: "We made punch and indulged in eating oysters by exchanging them while already holding them in our mouths. She would offer me hers, held on her extended tongue, while I would gently push mine into her mouth; there can be no more exciting and sensual a game between two lovers."

What is interesting in Casanova's love memoirs is less the boudoir pornographic content, than the way he describes Venice; the city's convents, alleyways, gardens and gondolas form the locations of his narrative. Reality and fiction merge into a sensual imaginary world, where the Serenissima is the backdrop used by Casanova to depict nuns who are anything but chaste, desirable courtesans, and festive masked balls as hubs of decadence.

Today, the Murano convent lies in ruins. Still, in Santa Maria degli Angeli on Fondamenta Venièr at least the church of the convent where M.M. must have lived is preserved. To this day, thanks to Casanova's frivolous sensuality, M.M. has remained a synonym for the male fantasy of the "Venus in the Convent" – and what other nun can boast this kind of title?

Address Statue "Vitae", Viale Bressagio, Murano, 30141 Venice | **Vaporetto fermata** Faro, line 3, 4.1/4.2, 7, 12, 13, 18, night route N | **Tip** Another point of interest here is the church of San Canciano, located near Fondamenta Nuove, where the boats to and from Murano arrive and depart; the church served as the location to arrange their secret encounters.

7__ The Tree Trunk
Commemorating the patron saint

The island of San Francesco del Deserto is not only an extraordinarily beautiful place – surely one of the most beautiful in Venice, but also a particularly historic one, as it was here in the northern lagoon that the history of the city began, with the first settlements of the islands.

Archaeological finds have shown that San Francesco del Deserto has been inhabited at least since the 1st century AD. The island owes its name to the Italian patron saint, Francis of Assisi, on the one hand, and also to the fact that living conditions became very inhospitable, due to climate changes, rising sea levels and a malaria epidemic. In the 15th century the island was even given up and abandoned for a period of over 20 years.

The silence and charm the cypress-covered island exudes doesn't reveal itself on one of the available guided daytime tours leaving from Burano. In order to really feel San Francesco del Deserto, the best thing to do is to stay for a few days and live and pray together with the monks – though, at least in theory, you have to be prepared for the Franciscans to hold prayers a total of seven times a day.

Those wanting to experience this peace and solitude should come in autumn or winter, which has the additional advantage that you won't be badgered by the countless mosquitoes that roam the island in the summer.

The island's Franciscan history begins in the year 1220. On his return from the Orient, Saint Francis dropped anchor here and is said to have stayed until 1224. According to legend, he planted a tree, which unfortunately was knocked down in an 18th-century storm. While the main trunk is kept in a cave only accessible to the monks, a small part is exhibited in the chapel dedicated to Fra Bernardino.

Address Chapel dedicated to Fra Bernhard, the tree trunk standing to the right on a wall, Isola di San Francesco del Deserto, 30100 Venice | **Opening times** By appointment Tue–Sun 9–11am and 3–5pm – there are just under 30 rooms available, and couples have to sleep in separate quarters; for bookings (in Italian) call tel. 0039/415286863 or email sfdeserto@libero.it | **Vaporetto fermata** The best way to get there is by private boat or to ask to be picked up by a monk in Burano after making arrangements by telephone. | **Tip** Enjoy unforgettably beautiful views of the surrounding lagoon from the various viewpoints set up on the island. Particularly mystical experiences are provided by the island in the moonlight during the autumnal fogs over the lagoon, creating a mysterious atmosphere.

8_ The Privy

A rather unchaste convent

There is a small island between Murano and Burano known as San Giacomo in Paludo. The building on the island is a pointer to its colorful history.

As early as 1046, the monastery of San Giacomo Maggiore was set up here as a place that pilgrims could venture to. In 1238 it was transferred to Cistercensian nuns, who moved to Torcello in 1440, however.

In 1456 the convent became a field hospital for lepers, and was subsequently restored by the Franciscans in the 16th century. In the 18th century the island became increasingly depopulated, until eventually only a lone secular mendicant was living on it, wielding a stick with an attached collection box, hoping for some alms from passing boats. The convent was eventually demolished in 1810, before the Austrians converted the complex into barracks, which also served as a military post for the Italians, up until 1961. What is interesting in this context is the bay window: this was a predecessor of our "water closet" – well, a seaside privy.

There are some spicy details to add to this. We know from Casanova and his contemporaries that in the Middle Ages the convents, in particular, were anything but places of chastity – to the contrary, the orgies staged there were so debauched that they would have made modern onlookers blush.

To this day, Venetian fishermen tell in hushed tones of the Paludo nuns who once used to stand with their skirts pulled up, attracting the attention of travellers by masturbating, either to shock them or to lure them into the convent, Sirens-style. Even given that there'll be a fair share of seaman's yarn, remember that every legend contains a kernel of truth and if fornication didn't happen here, then surely somewhere?

Address San Giacomo in Paludo | Vaporetto fermata While the island has a pier, for most of the year it is not accessible. However, you may spot the bay from the Murano-Mazzorbo boat. | Tip The small island of Sant'Andrea has an old fort, providing easy surveillance of the entrance from the Adriatic into the lagoon. Here, too, Casanova spent some time, not as a suitor, but as a prisoner. In 1743 he was under arrest here for a few months under the orders of Abate Grimani.

9__The Maze

Borges' wonderfully real-surreal world

The Abbey of San Giorgio Maggiore is remarkable, both from a historical (see page 28) and an artistic perspective. The Fondazione Giorgio Cini conducts research on art history here and exhibits an important part of its art collection at this location as well. What is particulary impressive is the courtyard of the monastery; as if Venice wasn't already one great inscrutable maze, it was given an artfully designed green labyrinth in 2012.

To commemorate the 25th anniversary of the passing of Argentinian writer, Jorge Luis Borges (1899–1986), who became famous for his work on the maze, a third cloister was created in the courtyard, between the Palladio cloister and the cypress cloister. This is a detailed reconstruction of the garden maze designed by the architect, Randoll Coate, in the 1980s, in honour of Borges and inspired by "The Garden of Forking Paths", one of Borges' most famous stories.

At over a kilometre in length, it consists of 3250 box trees designed to look like an open book, with Borges' name spelled out across the pages.

One of the most interesting aspects is a reference made to the author's blindness: visually-impaired visitors are led through the maze by a hand rail and may read one of Borges' stories in Braille.

Signs and symbols dear to the author – a walking stick, a mirror, an hourglass, sand, a tiger and a huge question mark – are part of this complex project, allowing a fine glimpse into Borges' fantastical world of real and fictitious elements, with recurring themes of infinity and time.

The declared goal was not only to create a garden of remembrance of the author, but also to fill it with spiritual thought – talk about literally getting lost in a literary work of art!

Address In the court of the Abbey of San Giorgio Maggiore, Isola di San Giorgio, 30133 Venice (best seen from the campanile of the monastery) | Opening times May–Sept Mon–Sat 9.30am–12.30pm and 2.30–6.30pm, Sun 2.30–5pm; Oct–April Mon–Sat 9.30am–12.30pm and 2.30pm–dusk, Sun 8.30–11am and 2.30pm–dusk | Vaporetto fermata San Giorgio, line 2, night route N | Tip In the park behind the abbey (not publicly accessible) you will discover the unique Teatro Verde, an amphitheatre open towards the sea, with unique rows of seats featuring backrests made of plants – hence the name "Green Theatre". It's only accessible to visitors of the theatre and during concert events held here in the summer (www.liveinve.com).

10_ The Statue of San Giorgio
Why the gondolier is a dragon slayer

A side room of the church of San Giorgio shelters a fine statue of Saint George, the legendary dragon slayer, who was to give his name to the island. Dating back to the 16th century, the statue was heavily damaged during a storm and was only restored with the support of the Swarovski Foundation. Saint George, however, is one of the most important emblematic figures of both the city of Venice and of the gondolier.

The term "gondola" appears for the first time in 1094 as "gondulam", in a decree by Doge Falier, probably deriving from the Latin "cymbula" (small boat) or "cuncula" (conch). According to legend, a dragon (or crocodile, see page 144) hides in the depths of the lagoon. The only living beings it is afraid of are the gondoliers, as their oars represent a threat to the monster, and the rudders symbolise the lancet used by Saint George to finish off the dragon. The lagoon sinking into dense fog is thus the breath of the dragon snorting with anger, yet not daring to surface for fear of the gondolier, constantly guarding the water.

It is by no means a coincidence that this small island was called San Giorgio Maggiore, as the prayers of the monks were supposed to calm the raging monster. The shape of the gondolas, too, is full of symbolism, reminiscent of the crescent moon, which the city of Venice feels a connection with. Last but not least, the choice of red as the colour of the Serenissima was not completely arbitrary either, this being the iconographic colour of Saint George. According to a Venetian legend, the blood of the monster injured by the lance not only stained the coat of the saint red, but also the city. The wounded dragon then disappeared into the lagoon, which is why the colour red also stands for Venice's victory over evil, the apostasy and heresy symbolised by the dragon.

Address Basilica di San Giorgio Maggiore (the statue stands to the right of the main entrance in a separate area, to one side), Isola di San Giorgio, 30133 Venice, tel. 0039/ 415227827, email abbaziasangiorgio@gmail.com | **Opening times** May–Sept Mon–Sat 9.30am–12.30pm and 2.30–6.30pm, Sun 2.30–5pm; Oct–April Mon–Sat 9.30am–12.30pm and 2.30pm–dusk, Sun 8.30–11am and 2.30pm–dusk | **Vaporetto fermata** San Giorgio, line 2, night route N | **Tip** San Giorgio was once the site of the only conclave for the papal election ever held in Venice, between 1 December 1799 and 14 March 1800. Venice was chosen because Rome was occupied by the French at the time and many cardinals had already fled to the city (Venice enjoyed the protection of Austria). A commemorative plaque in the famous Conclave Hall may be viewed during the guided tour.

11__ The Ossuary
The genesis of a bone island

The small island of Sant'Ariano lies to the north of the lagoon, northeast of Murano and Torcello in what is known as the "laguna morta" (see page 34). Coming over by boat today, the island doesn't exactly appear to be very inviting, and it's difficult to imagine that it was settled as early as somewhere around the year 500 when people from the city of Altino moved there. Around 1160 a convent with a church was built, and bridges were erected to make it easier to reach the neighbouring islands.

However, due to adverse weather and environmental issues, as well as rising sea levels, it became ever more difficult to access Sant'Ariano. Thus the decline of the convent started as early as around 1400, the last nuns moving away in 1439. By the early 16th century only ruins remained of the church and convent.

Around the 16th century, the Venetian health authorities came up with the idea of erecting an ossuary on the island, surrounded by a wall, for exhumed bodies. In 1565 the Senate agreed to this suggestion in order to relieve the pressure on the numerous small cemeteries within Venice called the "campielli dei morti" – putting a stop to the "wild burials" under the cobblestones of the alleyways. San Michele, which now serves as the central cemetery for Venice, was only established in 1837.

Today, the whole area is in a dilapidated state. Nearly entirely overgrown with bushes, shrubs and brambles, the ossuary is practically unreachable. While there is a boat jetty, it is hardly worth landing there, as the only visible reminder – the wall enclosing the ossuary – can be better viewed from the water, and the interior is not accessible, as the former gate has been walled up. However, they say that inside the ossuary the bones are still piled up several metres high.

Address Isola Sant'Ariano, 30142 Venice | **Getting there** With difficulty (see above, no public transport stop) | **Tip** A few years ago, a former cemetery was excavated on the island of Lazzaretto nuovo. A rumour was started that this was the "Cemetery of the Vampires", as a stone had been placed into the mouth of one woman, allegedly to stop her from sucking blood. However, it emerged that this was a hoax and the PR gag was quickly buried.

12__ The Vegetable Farm
Non solo castraure

Much has been written already about the "castraure" or artichokes of Sant'Erasmo; unfortunately not all of it is quite correct. First of all, it has to be said that there are various kinds of artichokes, and the type cultivated on Sant'Erasmo is not called "castraure", but "Violetto di San'Erasmo", the violet artichoke of Sant'Erasmo. Artichokes of this kind have been grown for centuries in the Venetian lagoon – not only on Sant'Erasmo, but also on other islands as well.

The reason why this vegetable thrives here is due to the local conditions. Artichokes love rough soil, such as is found on Sant'Erasmo, which is actually mud from the canals of the lagoon mixed with regular soil, which is now so fertile that farmers can usually get by without using fertilisers at all.

The word "castraure" specifically denotes the young fruit at the top of the plant, which has a pleasantly bitter taste and is usually enjoyed raw. The artichokes located at the next level down (just below the top), are known as "botoli" and are typically used in fish dishes or marinated in olive oil.

All the other fruits on the plant are the "carciofi", the artichokes proper as it were, and are much larger. These are usually processed into artichoke bottoms.

While artichokes do play an important role on the island, it would be wrong to reduce Sant'Erasmo to just this, as any kind of vegetable thrives here, something you can check out for yourself on a visit to the "I Sapori di Sant'Erasmo" vegetable farm. The island produces, not only wild asparagus, but also the famous and particularly tender and sweet lagoon peas, the vital ingredient of the classic Venetian "risi e bisi" risotto. Sant'Erasmo also has a long tradition of cultivating wine, with the ORTO estate enjoying a particularly good reputation.

Address Sapori di Sant'Erasmo, Via Boaria Vecia, 6 San Erasmo, 30141 Venice, tel. 0039/
415282997, www.isaporidisanterasmo.com | Getting there As the farm is slightly off the
beaten track, it's best to call and ask to be picked up or to rent a bike and ask for directions. |
Tip Also worth seeing is the Torre Massimiliano, erected during the Austro-Hungarian
empire, serving to block ships from entering the lagoon; today it is used as an arts centre.

13_ The Moleche
Soft shell – molto buono!

Torcello is a truly beautiful little spot. On rare clear days you can see all the way to the snow-capped mountain tops of the Karnish Alps. North of the island marks the beginning of what is known as the "laguna morta" (dead lagoon), comprising mainly fresh water and hardly affected by the tides. The part of the lagoon where water levels sink and rise with the tides is accordingly called "laguna viva" (living lagoon).

If humankind hadn't intervened, the lagoon would soon have become a deep water basin and the beautiful sandbanks and saltmarshes (barene), making up the landscape of the lagoon, would have literally disappeared.

The responsibility for this lies with the Lion City. It once had many small rivers that flowed into the lagoon, which were instead diverted to run straight into the Adriatic, to prevent the silting-up of the lagoon and to maintain the natural protection provided by the surrounding water.

The northern part of the island has a type of canal where you can make a special kind of trap. These are baskets used for catching specific types of shellfish. While the lagoon's crustaceans are usually protected by a hard carapace, this turns soft at certain times of the year, enabling the creatures to shed their skin. The males change their carapace twice a year – in spring and autumn – the females only once, in the autumn. The carapace-less soft crayfish are considered a true delicacy and are a popular prey for the fishermen.

The female crustaceans, called "manzaneta", are boiled and marinated for the "Insalata di mare". The much sought-after males, known as "moleche" in the Venetian dialect, are dipped into whisked egg, dusted with flour and deep fried in hot oil, which turns them into a delicacy called "moleche ripiene".

Address Torcello (canal above the Museo di Torcello), Isola di Torcello | Vaporetto fermata Torcello, linc 9, 12, night route N | Tip A good place to indulge crayfish cravings is the Trattoria da Romano (www.daromano.it) in Burano – by the way, this is also the place to sample the famous "risotto de gó" (with goby fish) or "risotto nero di sepia" (with octupus ink).

14_ The Ponte del Diavolo

Where the devil waits for eternity

Due to its picturesque location, the Ponte del Diavolo (Devil's Bridge) is one of the most-photographed locations on the island. Any visitor must pass it, by necessity, and no one is immune to the charm of this bridge – yet hardly anyone knows about the legend that provides the background to this magical place.

At the time of the Austrian occupation, a girl from a noble Venetian family fell in love with an Austrian officer. When the impossible love affair was discovered, to cover its shame, the patrician family immediately whisked the young lady away from the city and the young officer was found stabbed to death, his murderer never caught. When the young woman found out about the death of her lover, she collapsed, whereupon a friend promised to reunite her with her dear departed.

The friend turned to an old sorceress who was able to conjure up the demon guarding the key for space and time. A meeting was arranged for 24 December on the bridge of Torcello, as at that moment in time the good spirits are busy elsewhere.

The sorceress went to the bridge and called the demon. Upon his arrival, she negotiated with him to hand over the key to space and time – promising him in return the souls of seven unbaptised newborn children within seven days' time. Driven by greed, the demon agreed to the deal. The sorceress received the key, threw it into the water below and the young officer soon appeared under the arch of the bridge. The lovers were reunited and went on to find happiness in another world.

Seven days later, the devil waited in vain for the sorceress, who had perished in a fire. Since then the demon has been prowling past the bridge every year on the 24th of December in the shape of a black cat, still waiting for those souls, for all eternity.

Address Ponte del Diavolo, Isola di Torcello, 30142 Venice | *Vaporetto fermata* Torcello, line 9, 12, night route N | Tip While the story about the girl from the patrician Venetian family and the Austrian officer is based on real events, the second big mystery of the island – what is known as the Throne of Attila, a seat carved out of the rock at the front, near the basilica – is the product of sheer imagination; the seat was a bishop's seat with no connection to Attila whatsoever.

15_ The People Mover
Construction eyesores

The island of Tronchetto was once a fallow landscape; today, artificial extensions created through drainage, have enlarged it to its current size of 18 hectares. Its warehouses, factories, ferry jetties and multi-story car park have made it a modern infrastructure hub for the city of Venice. Yet the island remains somewhat controversial.

One reason for this is that the central vegetable market will be expanded to include a fish market, as the current fish market on Rialto is being discontinued. For the vendors this will probably be quite handy, less so for the residents, and the tourists will lose an interesting sight, even though few of them actually buy any fish from Rialto.

The second controversial issue is what it known as the People Mover, which, starting at Stazione Tronchetto, connects the port and the Piazzale Roma via Stazione Marittima. Seen from the vaporetto, the railway track is reminiscent of a prehistoric dinosaur skeleton, more eccentric than beautiful – yet for the Venetians, parking their cars in the multi-story car park to go shopping, the connection is quite practical. The tourists from the cruise ships – which on average only spend four to five hours in Venice – can get into the city and back to port far faster as well. Whether this is necessarily a good thing or not is irrelevant, really.

Things are somewhat different with a project planned for the island of Sacca San Biagio: the Disney-style theme park would probably stop many modern-day "cruisaders" from even rushing through Venice, as plenty of them probably wouldn't even venture into the city centre at all, waylaid by the lightweight theatre performances, fast-food chains, Ferris wheels and other such amusement park fare. Well, Venice has always been a city of the eternal Carnival, "divertimenti" (entertainments) and lucre!

Address Stazione Tronchetto, Isola del Tronchetto, 30135 Venice | **Vaporetto fermata** Peoplemover (PM), Tronchetto ferry boat, line 17 | **Tip** By the way, architectural eyesores are nothing new in Venice, just think of the 1971 Cassa di Risparmio at Campo Manin or the sports hall designed in 1976 in a monumental Eastern Block "charm" style behind the Naval Museum. Even a Venice-themed amusement park has been done before; there was one in Vienna, a 19th-century theme park by the name of "Venice in Vienna" in the Prater, which provided light entertainment with artificial palaces, canals and gondolas – Ferris wheel and all.

16__ The Cemetery Museum

A none too pacific burial site

The history of Venice is closely connected with the restriction of the rights of its Jews. It all started in the 10th century when Jews were banned from travelling by boat, before they were eventually completely chased out of the city, settling in Mestre and on Terraferma instead.

From 1348 onwards, the Jews once again found their place within the community, as their services were required in the world of banking – however, their personal and economic liberties were limited by what was called "condotte". When a location to bury their dead was needed, the city assigned the Jews a site on the Lido, which – leaving aside the San Nicolò monastery – was completely overgrown virgin territory. Following some squabbling with the less-than-enthusiastic Benedictine monks, the contract for the establishment of a cemetery was signed on 25 September 1386 – the first headstone dating from 1389 bears the name "Samuel ben Shimson".

However, the cemetery was not destined to be a peaceful place. First the Benedictines of San Nicolò had the graves defiled, then, during times of war, gravestones kept being removed and used to build fortifications, and, finally, flooding caused some of the graves to surface. The last burial on the "antico cimitero ebraico" took place in 1774 and then a new location, further inland, was taken into service, only to be razed eventually by Napoleon's troops.

While the old section is picturesque, it is more of a museum, than an actual cemetery – its grounds are not even those of the original site. And because of its troubled history, the link between the grave stones and their human remains has been broken – the bones can no longer be assigned to the right stone. This represents a particular humiliation for Jews, who view their graves as eternal.

Address Antico cimitero ebraico, Riviera San Nicolò, Lido, 30126 Venice | **Opening times** Only by appointment or during guided visits Sun–Fri 10am–4pm; for more information call tel. 0039/41715359 or email prenotazioni@codesscultura.it (Note: a guided tour costs the same for individuals or groups; the fee benefits the diminishing Jewish community of Venice) | **Vaporetto fermata** Lido S.ta Maria Elisabetta, line R, B, N, 1, 2, 5.1/5.2, 6, 8, 10, 14; on foot 10 minutes from the stop | **Tip** Walking past the entrance gate to the newer part of the Jewish cemetery and taking a left at the end into Via Marco Polo brings you to the Strada dietro l'Ospizio Marino, where the abandoned buildings of a former military hospital convey a ghostly oppressive atmosphere.

17___Icon on the Top Floor
The "birthplace" of Corto Maltese

Few people know that the top floor of the house at Via Doge 21 – the one with the splendid roof terrace – was home to none other than Hugo Pratt, who with his character, Corto Maltese, created a milestone within the international comic scene. Corto Maltese – which translates as the Small Maltese – appeared for the first time in 1967 in the series "Una Ballata del Mare Salato" (A South Sea Ballad), which takes place just before and during World War I, as he fights both pirates and the navies of both the German Reich and Great Britain in the Pacific. This melancholic adventure story is considered the starting point for European graphic novels.

Corto Maltese's name can be seen as a homage to Malta's independence. He is an eminently colorful figure, with many typically Mediterranean characteristics – an anarchistic, ironic and a stubborn soul, a seaman without a ship, and a romantic hero. His travels lead him to all continents, but these travels are no mere treasure hunts, but more of a search for himself. As an idealised self-portrait, he was to become the main character in Pratt's work.

In the Corto Maltese stories, fascinating and fabulously beautiful ladies play an important role; this is one of the main reasons that the fan base of this dreamy, nihilistic and capricious womaniser mainly consists of adults.

Following the publication of these novels, the Serenissima, too, was gripped by the charm of the Maltese stories. Today, you can feel this magic in the Corto Maltese Museum, at the Corte Sconta restaurant in Calle del Pedistrin alla Bragora, at Campiello Corto Maltese – which has now been dedicated to our seafarer, and in the Hotel Sofitel (its owner was a friend of Pratt's). However, the most significant location is the house on the Lido, where Corto Maltese was born.

Address Via Doge, Lido 21 the top floor of the building; the roof terrace enjoys a sea view), Malamocco, 30126 Venice | Opening times Private residence, the apartment cannot be visited (only viewed from the outside) | Vaporetto fermata Lido S.ta Maria Elisabetta, line R, B, N, 1, 2, 5.1/5.2, 6, 8, 10, 14; also easily reached by bus from Piazzale S. Maria Elisabetta in the direction of Alberoni | Tip The hotel that keeps cropping up in Corto Maltese's stories is the Trattoria da Scarso in Malamocco, Piazzetta di Malamocco, where Hugo Pratt enjoyed meeting his friends; our recommendation, however, would be the Trattoria Ai Ponte di Borgo in Calle delle Mercerie no. 27.

18__ The Anchors

A blessing in disguise ... or maybe not?

At the corner of the Sotoportego del Traghetto, you'll discover two double hooks resembling an anchor cemented into the wall. Many passing by will touch these or bang them against the wall – it's meant to bring good luck, which is a strange and eccentric custom once you know the history of these hooks.

You see, they were once a bloody part of the Venetian justice system. The "promissio maleficiorum" (criminal law) was not exactly squeamish, with regards to capital punishment, in particular for murder, robbery combined with manslaughter, and the sexual abuse of children. A criminal needed not only to be punished, but vengeance had to be as gruesome as the crime committed. Alongside the less harmful penalties, such as pillory, branding, flogging and banishment from the city, more horrific crimes resulted in eyes being gouged out, ears cut off, hands chopped off or a spell in the dungeon. The next step up was the death penalty, with methods ranging from "simple" hanging, drowning and bludgeoning to beheading and burning to death.

However, if a crime was particularly serious as well as uncommonly heinous and treacherous, things were taken one step further, by combining various punishments. In such cases the criminal would first be publicly jeered before being taken to the place where the crime had occurred, where his hands would be chopped off. After that he would be dragged to the hangman, beaten and flogged all the while – and tortured using all the methods in the book, before the pronouncement of the verdict. Eventually the body would be quartered and exhibited at four different locations around the city – and the individual body parts would be hung from hooks such as the ones mentioned here. Sadly, the question as to why they supposedly bring good luck remains unanswered.

Address Corner of the Sotoportego del Traghetto, at the estuary of the Ponte San
Canciano into Calle de la Malvasia, 30121 Venice | Vaporetto fermata Ca' D'oro, line 1,
night route N | Tip The two rings hanging from the wall at the back of the building –
known as "sciavonéle" – were used to fasten the chains of the pillory, where the
condemned man was exposed to the jeers of the citizenry.

19__The Bigoli

Venice's contribution to pasta

While you can see pasta dishes on menus nearly everywhere in Venice, it should be noted that pasta is more of a tribute to the culinary preference of tourists and their expectations of Italian cuisine, rather than typically Venetian. The Venetians themselves are traditionally more partial to risotto dishes.

Still, there is one regional pasta variation in Venice that is hard to find in its original version. We are talking about the bigoli, a specific type of "pasta lunga" (long pasta, like spaghetti). As Stefano Aldreghetti of Ristorante da Poggi explains, "Bigoli are a local and very aromatic type of pasta made from wheat or buckwheat dough and plenty of eggs – the original recipe uses duck eggs. In the past, before pasta machines and industrial production dominated the market, pasta – noodle by noodle – was exclusively rolled out by hand. At a later date, a kind of rustic pasta press called a bigolaro was introduced. Attached to a stool, it consisted of a brass tube with a bronze mold inside it, which pressed into the dough while someone turned a cranked handle. However, this is not truly original, as bigoli are a particularly thick pasta of an authentic irregular shape which can only be created by hand." As this is very labour intensive, the pasta was produced by the community as a whole and allowed to dry on a bed of dried cane.

Bigoli are best served as "pasta fresca" (fresh pasta), either as "bigoli in salsa" (with onion and salty sardines), as "bigoli alla pescatora" (with clams, prawns and/or calamari), or in the shape of the famous "bigoli con ragù d'anatra". With the latter, the bigoli is first served with the wild duck sugo sauce as a "primo" and the boiled duck meat is enjoyed afterwards as a "secondo".

To sample this typically Venetian cuisine, Ristorante da Poggi is a great choice.

Address Ristorante da Poggi, Rio terra' Maddalena, Cannaregio, 30121 Venice, tel. 0039/41721199 | **Opening times** Tue–Sun 12.30–2.30pm and 7–11pm | **Vaporetto fermata** San Marcuola, line 1, night route N | **Tip** A good location for buying fresh top-quality pasta is the Casa del Parmigiano, San Polo 214.

20__Blucobalto

The wonderful world of Pietro Russo

There has never exactly been a shortage of artists in Venice, in fact, if anything, there are far too many to keep track of. Some are big names, while others shine with well-known works, yet at Campo dei Mori you'll find an artist who doesn't fit into any of the art clichés, but creates his own style somewhere between the real and the surreal. His name is Pietro Russo – and he calls his work "Blucobalto".

It's a world of imagination that Pietro Russo, originally from Naples, has created here, rather than a world of provocation or protest; he also doesn't seem interested in redefining art. Russo's drawings, bronze sculptures, works in wood and furniture are alive.

Viewers become a part of this daydream, where birds feast in blissful gardens at the eternal bosom of sensual mother figures, where angel-like archers gaze at imaginary faraway destinations full of longing, where mythological horses meet happy sheep, where Sirens hover over the water and young women dance and frolic with fish.

Observers feel as if they have returned to an archaic place, a past paradise even, and are tempted to think of Atlantis and all the charming allegories connected with this mythical world.

And yet, this delightful scenery is not pure mythology or fantasy. Pietro has absorbed the external world and is now describing his own personal experiences and feelings; his work is a testament to his close connection to art and its history, claiming its divine origins in ancient times. If dream and reality then blend into a comforting feeling of well-being, as one has probably only ever experienced at the nourishing breast of one's mother, in this wondrous moment his art appears to appeal to the viewer for something empathy.

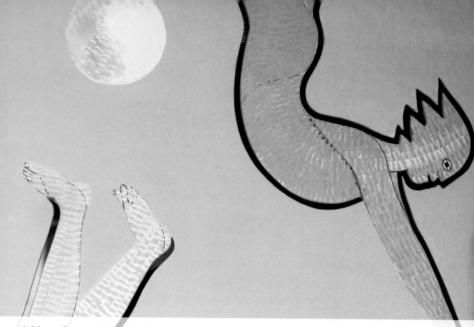

Address Campo dei Mori, Cannaregio 3384, 30121 Venice (www.pietrorusso.it) | **Opening times** Visits are possible by appointment, tel. 0039/3471525044 | **Vaporetto** fermata Orto, line A, 4.1/4.2, 5.1/5.2 | **Tip** At the corner of Campo dei Mori and Fondamenta Mori, the Ostaria L'Orto dei Mori may not be able to offer a fairytale world, but it does seduce one's palate with sumptuous down-to-earth cuisine and wine – which is worth a lot too! (www.osteriaortodeimori.com)

21_ The Crown of Flames

Alchemy in the Philosophers' House

In alchemy, the borders between charlatanism and philosophy were not always clearly defined. While all alchemists were people with a comprehensive education, many of them lacked moral fibre. Others had an inherent balance between intellect and the heart; moral principles, culture, penance and modesty – which is what really made the alchemist a philosopher, as "spiritual alchemy" had only one true goal, illumination.

This is very different from what made alchemy famous, i.e. the "magic" in the laboratory with the aim of turning ordinary metals into silver or gold.

In principle, the two strands were not considered separate; the alchemist would humbly reproduce the sublime universe in the laboratory, turning into a spiritual alchemist once outside his laboratory. Those who dedicated themselves to the production of silver and gold became charlatans.

Venice was teeming with real alchemists, but there were a few con artists amongst them too, who used tricks to swindle their fellow citizens, damaging the reputation of alchemy in the process. A particularly popular prop here was a wooden box with a double floor where gold was hidden, appearing at the opportune moment. To end the fraud, alchemists were subjected to the death penalty from 1530 onwards.

In an effort to escape this threat, while guarding their secrets, the spiritual alchemists began to develop a symbolic and metaphoric language only understood by the initiated. The King of Flames, on one of the reliefs on the Palazzo Lezze, represents the living gold and the soul's search for awareness through the sun. Which is probably why the French philosopher and alchemist, Fulcanelli, called the palace the "Philosophers' House".

Address Palazzo Lezze, Fondamenta della Misericordia, Cannaregio 3598, 30121 Venice |
Vaporetto fermata S. Marcuola, line 1, night route N | **Tip** A little further along at Fonda-
menta Misericordia, the Vino Vero wine bar is a good spot to enjoy imaginatively prepared
cicchetti, such as "dentice mantecato" (dentex puree, similar to "baccala mantecato"),
courgette carpaccio with a mint pesto, rucola with fish marinated in olive oil and raw
marinated mushrooms with pancetta – good wine and a pleasant clientele make this bar
a place of sheer pleasure!

22__ The Eruv

An unusually modern interpretation

Threatened by persecution in Spain and Portugal, and endangered by the League of Cambrai, who were on a campaign against Venice – the Terraferma territories in particular, many Jews fled to Venice.

As everywhere else in Europe, Jews were subjected to restrictions here – they were tolerated as medics or bankers, but not as citizens. Indeed, they were most valued for the money they brought into the city. When the Venetian-led banks collapsed around 1500, the Jews were given a right of residence in the city.

On 29 March 1516, the Senate issued a law whereby they were allowed to live in the area of the iron founders – or "getori" – thus creating the first ghetto. Looking at a map of Venice, you'll see why this particular area was chosen – it was easily detached from the rest of the city.

On the ground floor of the Spanish Synagogue, visitors encounter a strange map showing the borders of what was known as the Eruv.

The Eruv refers to an Old Testament tradition, whereby Jews were prohibited from carrying any item from one public place to another on the Shabbat and on Yom Kippur.

Taken literally, the law is very strict, as one is allowed to carry neither a key nor a pair of glasses (except on the nose), biros or any other items of daily life.

To get around this rule, the Jewish community of Venice came to an agreement with the city council – not without paying a "modest" fee – whereby some public areas were now considered the private property of the Jewish community, exempting them from this ban.

This modern interpretation of the old custom allowed Jews to carry items on their person in this designated area.

Address Spanish Synagogue, Campo del Ghetto Vecchio, Cannaregio, 30121 Venice | **Opening times** During services (Friday evenings, Saturday at 9am) only guided visits | **Vaporetto fermata** Guglie, line A, 4.1/4.2 and 5.1/5.2 | **Tip** At the entrance of the two houses leading into the old ghetto, you can still see the holes which held the door hinges of the gates to the ghetto, which were closed at nightfall. After midnight, no Jew was allowed to leave the ghetto. The discrimination was only lifted under the Napoleonic administration, which had the gates burned.

23__ The Gentlemen from the East

Just off the Campo

A little off the beaten track, the Campo dei Mori is well-known for its three stone figures representing the brothers Sandi, Afani and Rioba Mastelli. Despite the name of the Campo, the brothers were natives of Morea, on the Greek Peloponnese.

The rich merchants arrived in Venice in 1112 and had the Palazzo Mastelli built across the way. The palace is also known as Palazzo del Cammello, owing to a relief showing a merchant with a camel laden with wares. Their wealth, as well as their far-reaching commercial network, even secured the Mastelli family a seat in the Great Council.

The statue showing Rioba Mastelli, in particular, catches the eye because of its iron nose. For a long time people believed this to be a symbol of wealth; in truth, this is merely a replacement for the original stone nose, which was lost. According to legend, the brothers turned into stone, as the result of a curse, and now have to stay here for eternity, as a deterrent for greed. Even so, in true Italian style, rubbing the iron nose is said to bring good luck.

The Campo certainly doesn't owe its name "dei mori" to the Moors. Yet a little off the Campo, in a niche in a house at the Fondamenta Mori – opposite the Palazzo Mastelli – you will find the statue of an elegantly dressed man with a splendid turban. For a long time it was claimed that this was a servant of the Mastelli brothers, but that is highly improbable – who would have erected such a monument to a servant?

To this day it is not clear who the mysterious statue really is, which has left a lot of room for speculation, including suggestions that it might be Marco Polo himself.

Address Fondamenta Mori, Cannaregio 3398, 30131 Venice | Vaporetto fermata Orto, line A, 4.1/4.2 and 5.1/5.2 | Tip Above and to the right of the statue a simple commemorative plaque reminds us that the famous painter Tintoretto passed away in this house in 1594.

24_ Gouged-out Eyes
Served on a tray

The Corner Cappella in the church of Santi Apostoli is home to a relatively unknown Tiepolo painting, with the fine name of "La Comunione di Santa Lucia" (The Communion of Saint Lucia). Normally, Holy Communion is supposed to be a day of celebration, yet this picture tells of the martyrdom of Saint Lucia and of how she received her last communion before being executed.

According to legend, Lucia was born to a wealthy noble family in 300 AD in Syracuse. Disappointed by her bridegroom, she decided to dedicate her life to God and took a vow of chastity and poverty, distributing her bridegroom's fortune amongst the poor. Furious, the rejected man denounced her as a Christian to the consul, Paschasius, further adding that Lucia had broken the Emperor's laws.

After trying in vain to persuade Lucia to negate God, the consul ordered a few of his guards to rape the young woman and to take her into a brothel to have her defiled by force. But the Holy Spirit descended upon Lucia and made her so heavy that not even a dozen oxen, together with the men, were able to move her. To put a stop to this "witchcraft", the consul ordered his henchmen to pour first urine and then boiling hot tar and oil mixed with resin over her. For reasons that aren't clear, the consul desisted from his plan and instead ordered that Lucia's eyes be gouged out before decapitating her.

It is this scene which is represented in the painting, in a very spectacular if also macabre way, with Lucia's eyes lying cut out on a tray with the bloodied carving knife alongside them.

According to legend, Lucia, whose name means "light", put her eyes back in before being decapitated and was able to see once more. She thus became the patron saint of opticians and is invoked for eye complaints.

Address Capella Corner in the church of Santi Apostoli, Campo Santi Apostoli, Cannaregio, 30121 Venice | **Vaporetto fermata** Ca' d'Oro, line 1, night route N | **Tip** The painting "Il Martirio di Santa Lucia" (The Martyrdom of Saint Lucia), which is on display in the church of Giorgio Maggiore, Isola di San Giorgio Maggiore, shows the scene when oxen and men tried in vain to move Lucia to her place of execution. The relics of the saint are kept in the church of Santi Geremia e Lucia, Campo San Geremia.

25__The Inscription

A "frosty" stone

As far back as the 15th century, the Venetians diverted the main rivers the Brenta, Piave and Sile into the Adriatic, to prevent mud, sand and fresh water from silting up the lagoon (see page 34). These mighty efforts were an expression of an ideology of superiority and independence – after all, as there was no connection to territories on the mainland, one was nobody's subject. In the eyes of Venice, its neighbours were first and foremost potential enemies, whose intrusion needed to be prevented; the surrounding water and the confusing web of canals provided a good level of protection.

However, there were years when this protection turned into a threat, and how close this threat could come became clear, most of all, in extremely cold winters, when the lagoon would freeze over, opening up a possibility for enemies to come across the ice to conquer Venice. According to old documents, this would have well been possible in the winter of 1431/32, yet none of the city's adversaries took advantage of this opportunity. Over the last centuries, other winters have remained etched in people's memories for being exceptionally cold: in 1708, 1789, 1864 and 1929, for instance, the lagoon was completely frozen over – yet without political fallout.

A pillar on Sotoportego del Traghetto bears an interesting inscription, penned by a certain, Vincenzo Bianchi: "To the eternal memory of the year 1864, when Venice froze solid and people walked from the Fondamenta Nuova to the island of San Cristoforo, forming a long queue."

The lagoon had such a thick cover of ice that winter, that people were able to wander across the ice all the way to the island of San Cristoforo (today connected with San Michele). It doesn't bear thinking about what would have happended if a rival power had gone the opposite direction and marched on Venice.

Address Sotoportego del Traghetto (former cloisters), Cannaregio, 30121 Venice | **Vaporetto fermata** Ca"D'oro, line 1, night route N | **Tip** The nearby church of San Canciano, Campo San Canciano, is also well worth a visit – particularly as it presents a very plain design, completely atypical for Venice. Most of all this is due to the fact that the restoration planned for the 15th century was pushed forward to the 18th century, due to lack of funds. The church is close to the Santi Apostoli Canal, formerly an important traffic artery for boats from Istria and the nearby islands of Torcello, Mazzorbo, Burano and Murano.

26___The Letterbox

A "bocca della verita" for informers

As a consequence of the Tiepolo Conspiracy (see page 204), one of
the most powerful political bodies of all times was created in July
1310: the Consiglio dei Dieci, the mystical Council of Ten. Initially
it was given authority over policing and security in order to completely uncover the multi-tentacled conspiracy. Originally two months
were scheduled for this operation, with an extension of two months
if more time was needed.

In 1455, with people probably tiring of these eternal security forces,
the Council of Ten was nonetheless elevated to the status of a permanent institution, the highest security authority in Venice, no less.
The Maggior Consiglio would select the members of the Council
from amongst the Senate, sessions only taking place in the presence
of the Doge.

The Consiglio dei Dieci was responsible for protecting the state,
maintaining public order, preventing espionage and uncovering con-
spiracies and high treason. Becoming ever-more powerful, the Council soon enjoyed unlimited legal powers, from torture and persecution
to secret bank accounts all the way to sanctioned assassinations. Further controlling the regulatory body, the superior court of law, as well
as taking over the war ministry, allowed the Council of Ten to become a kind of super ministry. Spying and covert investigations were
the order of the day, creating a regime of domestic terror.

One source of information was letterboxes, such as the one on
a brick wall in Cannaregio. This is where informers were able to
throw bits of paper with their accusations into the slot. They did not
have to fear reprisals; while they did have to sign the accusations by
name, this was kept secret by the Council of Ten. No wonder, then,
that the Council was soon able to count on a whole army of paid
spies.

Address Calle della Testa, Cannaregio 6216, 30121 Venice | Vaporetto fermata Ospedale, line B, 4.1/4.2, 5.1/5.2, 22 | Tip Another fine example of this kind of letterbox can be found in the Loggia of the Palazzo Ducale. By the way: when the Council of Ten became too powerful, even for the city fathers' liking, its powers were limited again; at the same time the "Avogadori del Comùm", from the 14th century onwards, were starting to emerge as a pillar for the rule of law, ensuring that office holders respected the laws and didn't go beyond their remit. They were also able to appeal against decisions of the infamous Council of Ten.

27__Marco Polo

A very lively bookshop

No, this isn't a treatise on the question of whether Signore Polo made it to China or not. Still we should mention that Marco Polo was not only quite an argumentative fellow, but also commanded a Venetian galley in the sea war against Genova, which is often somewhat forgotten amongst all his tales of adventure. Falling into Genovese hands during the sea battle at Curzola, he passed the time until his release regaling others with his exploits.

For its part, the Marco Polo Bookshop, which specialises in travel, also has a lot of stories to tell; while these might be less exciting than Polo's, they are a testament to hard realities no less difficult to navigate than travel adventures. For instance, the small, not exactly cash-rich bookshop was handed a fine of 1000 euros by the Office of Public Works responsible for maintaining the allure of Venice, only because the shop had put up a poster advertising an event (two sheets of A4 paper) without a permit.

Fair enough, the law is the law, you could say – yet where is the sense of proportion, given the oversized advertising hoardings on the scaffoldings of the bridges and palazzi? It looks like a preoccupation with city blight cannot compete with the city authorities' love of filled coffers.

The Venetians are patient and take a lot in stride, especially if they don't lose out commercially they can work around the "touristic fundamentalism", in the wise words of the Venetian writer, Tiziano Scarpa. If it becomes too much, they look for new ways, just like Marco Polo once did.

So, it now looks like this bookshop will find a new path – with vegetables: once a week (on Wednesdays) the premises serve as a distribution hub for organic vegetable boxes (well, bags) from San Erasmo. New paths, indeed.

Address Marco Polo Bookshop, Cannaregio 5886/A, 30121 Venice, Tel. 0039/415226343, www.libreriamarcopolo.com | **Opening times** Mon–Thu and Sat 9.30am–7.30pm, Fri 9.30–11am | **Vaporetto fermata** Rialto, line A, 1, 2, night route N | **Tip** As his contemporaries didn't believe Marco Polo's stories, he acquired the nickname Messer Millione – a reminder of this still in existence today is the Corte del Milion, right behind the Chiesa di San Giovanni Crisostomo in Cannaregio, where Marco Polo's house used to stand.

28___ The Nymph with Two Satyrs

Mythology is a matter for interpretation

Venice and eroticism is a truly endless subject. Walking the city with your eyes peeled, you'll see not only nude figures (usually female) in every nook and cranny, but also explicit references to desire and physical love – they are everywhere, from the Doge's Palace, to churches and museums, as well as on the facades of houses.

One example, a seemingly frivolous house decoration, can be found in Cannaregio, where a balcony is adorned with the representation of a nymph "encircled" by two satyrs. The female figure is intertwined in ivy and vine leaves, identifying her as a maenad or a nymph; she is also carrying a basket of fruit on her head. The two satyrs, their lower halves resembling goats, are represented as children suckling on the nymph's bosom, embraced by her as if by a mother. In the two top corners you can make out a small child.

Part human, part goat, the satyrs are usually represented as ithyphallic (i.e. with an erection) and as sexually uninhibited; always up for it and willing to cross the border into rape if their desire is not satisfied. While nymphs are in principle lesser demi-goddesses, they are considered (with a few exceptions) to this day as synonymous with female desire.

Still, if you look closely you'll see that the scene represented here is not – as is usually the case with nymphs and satyrs – a sign of exaggerated sex drive and orgiastic debauchery, but tells the story of a fertility ritual. The message it conveys is more about a certain female dominance; for one, the female figure is over double the size of the two satyrs, and for another, she is holding them in the manner of suckling babes.

So, this is probably not even a slice of salon pornography, but rather a more tongue-in-cheek comment on sexuality.

Address Rio Terrà San Leonardo, 1304 Cannaregio, 30121 Venice (on the first-floor balcony) | Vaporetto fermata San Marcuola, line 1, night route N | Tip At the nearby Campo della Maddalena, the eponymous church of della Maddalena catches the eye for its numerous masonic symbols – such as the "eye of God" above the entrance outside. Another conspicuous inscription on the façade is: "sapietia aedificavit sibi domum" (Wisdom has erected a House here), a phrase that seemingly relegates God to a lesser position, seemingly too secular, really, for a church.

29__ The Offertory Box

The battle between good and evil

Venice is scattered with outdoor sculptures and votive vessels mainly dating from the 9th or the 13th century. Bear in mind, however, that the existence of such antique bowls doesn't necessarily mean that the building dates from that era, as many of these older pieces were worked into more recent constructions.

Most of the them are a testimony to the eternal fight between good and evil, and the offertory box in the church of Santa Maria Assunta, featuring two eagles, each catching a hare in their talons, is no exception.

Thanks to its two sets of eyelids, the eagle is the only bird that can look at the sun, making it a symbol for spiritual elevation, as the sun is taken to represent Christ. The eagle's clutching of the hare represents both primal uncontrollable bodily instincts and the fight between good and evil.

There are two possible interpretations however: the hare may be viewed as a symbol of the human soul trying to save itself from persecution by the devil – which is represented by the eagle. Another analysis sees the eagle as a symbol for Jesus Christ, in which case the hare would stand for impurity and evil's fear of facing the light.

The aim is to free oneself from all evil – this can be done through the Eucharist and the sacrifice of Jesus Christ. This idea is depicted in other imagery as well – for instance the frequent representation of a pelican, as the symbol of Christ's sacrifice. The belief was that the pelican would sacrifice its own body to feed its brood (in fact it is feeding them with fish from its beak). The fish, of course, represent Christ; in Greek, fish is "ichthus", corresponding to the initials Ièsous Christos Théou Uios Sôtêr (Jesus Christ, Son of God, Saviour).

Address Chiesa di Santa Maria Assunta/I Gesuiti, Campo dei Gesuiti, Cannaregio, 30131 Venice (the offertory box is immediately to the right past the entrance) | Opening times daily 10am–12 noon and 4–6pm | Vaporetto fermata Fondamenta Nuove, line B, 4.1/4.2, 5.1/5.2, 12, 13, 22, night route N | Tip At the side entrance of the Carmini Church on Campo Santa Margherita in Dorsoduro, set into the wall to the right, you can see a fine example of a great variety of votive vessels.

30__ Orsoni

A library of colours

In existence since 1888, the Orsoni company is the last of its kind in the Old Town of Venice.

Its great merit is threefold: the preservation of the old traditional Byzantine mosaic technique, meeting new challenges with innovative ideas, and the upkeep of the widely unknown tradition of Murano enamel. Today, Orsoni produces mainly mosaic tiles from glass and leaf gold.

When one visits, they explain much of the processes involved in producing mosaic tiles, and it's noticeable how much of the production is still done the traditional way: the first step is the melting pot, where the raw materials are melted down to a white mass and subsequently tinted using different metal oxides. This is followed by what is known as the rullata, whereby the individual glass forms are created, while in the next step these are slowly and carefully cooled down to room temperature. Last, but not least, the sheets are cut, using a specific saw designed by company founder, Angelo Orsoni.

As the firm has always maintained a close connection with artists, since its inception, it has aimed to provide them with the broadest possible range of colour options. This was the basis for the establishment of the Biblioteca del Colore, the legendary Library of Colours, as early as 1889. The library houses an archive of over 3000 (!) different colour tones and shades, rendering practically any combination of colours possible.

Every day, thousands of gold leaf and enamel mosaic tiles leave the factory to be used all over the world. Thus, these glorious little stones grace the floor of Dresdner Bank in Frankfurt, as well as adorn the golden Buddha statue in Singapore, and cover the walls of the monastery of St Irene in Athens.

Address Calle Vitelli 1045, 30121 Venice, tel. 0039/4124400023, www.orsoni.com |
Opening times Visits only by previous appointment, email: info@orsoni.com | Vaporetto
fermata Guglie, line A, 4.1/4.2 und 5.1/5.2 | Tip Another firm famous for its colours is
Fortuny, purveyor of the finest fabrics – the factory, however, remains hidden from curious
visitors, as the production of the fabrics is subject to the strictest secrecy. But the garden
may be visited (www.fortuny.com), or simply head for the Sky roof bar of the Molino
Stucky, Giudecca, 810 – from there you'll also have a pleasant view of the garden.

31__ The Red Fourth Floor

Baron Corvo and the gondolieri

In the early 20th century an eccentric Englishman moved into the fourth floor of the Palazzo Marcello. Frederick William Rolfe – better known under his pseudonym Baron Corvo – was born in 1860 in London and left the home of his parents by the age of 15. One of the careers he pursued was that of a Catholic priest, but he was expelled from seminary school. Though that endeavor didn't take off, Frederic was so enamoured of church pomp that he had his flat in the palazzo clad with crimson fabric, a material used for the soutanes of the Cardinals.

One of the reasons he'd had to leave England was that he'd gotten into hot water for being homosexual; in the more tolerant Venice, he was able to live a bohemian life, living off of rich men and going swimming with young gondolieri.

While not very successful as a writer, he always managed to find sponsors who would finance his lifestyle. The eccentric "baron" with the cropped hair, pince-nez, pipe and chequered cap was known all over town.

Seeing that as a writer he was closer to starvation than fame and fortune, one fine day he had the idea to capitalise on his sexual orientation, becoming the author of gay pornographic literature and a pimp too, arranging alluring youngsters for rich homosexual Englishmen – business was lucrative, and from then on he didn't have to freeze or go hungry, but was free to enjoy his life in red pomp and circumstance.

On 25 October, 1913, Corvo was found dead in his flat, which had long been Venice's main topic of erotic gossip. They say the consul of His Majesty was very quick to remove the extensive collection of pornographic photographs, erotic drawings, musings, notes and compromising addresses.

Address Palazzo Marcello Duchessa di Berry, Canal Grande/Calle Erizzo, Cannaregio 2134, 30121 Venice | **Opening times** The palazzo may only be viewed from the outside. | **Vaporetto fermata** San Marcuola, line 1, night route N | **Tip** Unfortunately Corvo's cardinal-red flat may not be visited. The "Red Bathtub" pictured here stands, not in said Palazzo, but in the Vineria All'Amarone (Calle dei Sbianchesini, San Polo), where, filled with ice, it serves as a Prosecco cooler among other things. By the way, at Amarone's they also serve an excellent carpaccio of marinated Angus beef or aromatic canapés with pancetta, quail's egg and truffles.

32__ The Santa Lucia Plaque

The church demolished for a railway station

Every year, millions of people – probably both locals and tourists alike – walk across the commemorative plaque in the ground, knowingly or not. Indeed, this is a fairly inconspicuous reminder of the former church of Santa Lucia which once stood here. When the railway station was built, in 1861, the church was simply torn down. Today's railway station building was completed in 1952, its current appearance the result of a series of designs that emerged in the context of a 1934 competition. The competition's winner was a certain, Virgilio Vallot (1901–1982), yet the building was only completed long after the end of the war by architect, Paolo Perilli.

Incidentally, the railway line established in the mid-19th century between Vienna and Venice was the reason why Vienna's South Station once featured two St Mark's Lions – one was not to survive the bombing during the Second World War, the other still adorns the former entrance hall of the old South Station, which is currently being converted into Vienna's Central Station (in Vienna's new main railway station too, the Venetian lion occupies its position in the station hall).

Prior to building the railway station in Venice, several buildings were razed to the ground: the Scuola dei Nobili, the Palazzo Lion Cavazza, the aforementioned church of Santa Lucia (including its convent) and the church of Corpus Domini. Just think of what would happen if anyone were to propose such a preposterous idea today …

To allow the ongoing veneration of Saint Lucia and her relics, previously kept in the church torn down in 1861, the church of Santi Gremia was extended by one chapel and rechristened Santi Gremia e Lucia. The only reminders of the former is the commemorative plaque and the railway station itself, Stazione di Venezia Santa Lucia.

DEGLI AVI NEL 1313 ERESSE E DEDICC
A LA CHIESA RINNOVATA AGLI INIZI
L 1860

ALE DI SAN GEREMIA PROFETA C
ED CORPO DELLA MARTIRE C

Address The commemorative plaque is situated in the heart of the square in front of the entrance to the main station, Fondamenta Santa Lucia, Cannaregio, 30121 Venice | **Vaporetto fermata** Ferrovia, line 1, 2, 3, 4.1/4.2, 5.1/5.2, night route N | **Tip** A similar situation occurred in Giudecca, an area which had a number of factories. Near the station there was a match factory, Fiammiferi Saffa, which was very important up until the 1950s (today this area houses a block of flats in Calle Solfarin), and a spot near Piazzale Roma once housed the tobacco factory, Manifattura Tabacchi, at the time one of the largest industrial sites in Venice.

33__ The Terrazzo Veneziano
Advanced recycling

In this "long-term lab for lightweight construction", as Venice is often called, architects traditionally have tried to save on material whenever possible, to minimise the weight of the buildings – and it is exactly this which led to the surprising lightness of the buildings and the magic of the facades opening up towards the canal. The floors, too, had to fulfil specific requirements: to be waterproof, elastic and durable, as in Venice reconstructions are understandably rather difficult. Of course the floors needed to meet aesthetic requirements as well. All these conditions were satisfied by the "terrazzo veneziano", which when polished to a shine, reflects light and is able to lighten up the darkest rooms. The technology of the terrazzo was not developed in Venice, however, but in Old Byzance, where tile and marble leftovers were already recycled in this way.

Terrazzo veneziano is a true miracle material, able to resist the specific climatic conditions of the city, ranging from hot and dry to damp and moist, all the way to frosty and even freezing cold. The perhaps somewhat unpretentious floors of lime-bound marble stone (and other stone) may be produced in a vast range of colours and it is laid loosely, thus enabling it to adapt to the fluctuations caused by water, wind and gas bubbles working themselves free from the floor. However, there's one quality terrazzo certainly does not have, and that's skid-mark resistance.

Few individuals are left who still follow this traditional craft, as here, too, easier-to-handle synthetic industrial products have long since supplanted the old traditions – Roberto Patrizio's workshop is one of the last "terrazzini". As the propietor explains, "Blue is the most expensive terrazzo, as it's usually made from Swedish sodalite or Egyptian lapislazuli; this is something only the wealthiest patricians and the prelates were able to afford!"

Address Patrizio Attilio (S.N.C.), Fondamenta San Giobbe, Cannaregio 683, 30121 Venice, tel. 0039/41720023 | **Opening times** The bottega (workshop) is open during the usual days of the week, but may only be visited by previous appointment (or friendly enquiry). | **Vaporetto fermata** Tre Archi, line 5.1/5.2, 22 | **Tip** Worth a visit: the nearby Bar al Parliamento (Cannaregio 511), with an excellent Spritz al bitter and tasty Piadine – its best feature though is its informal ambience.

34_ The Tree Nursery
"Il Vivaio alla Misericordia"

Today, at the location where the Santa Maria della Misericordia convent once stood, you'll find an idyllic and atmospheric green space and the only tree nursery in the old town of Venice. Ancient walls shelter a lush garden filled with greenhouses, flowers and plants of all types – with the remains of the venerable Campanile Valverde jutting up amongst them.

The Cooperativa Sociale Laguna Fioritá works with the disabled, and runs the garden and looks after the cultivation of the plants which are marketed through direct sales. Nature lovers will have a field day here, as will gardeners – the cooperative has a great variety of gardening utensils, alongside plants of all kinds. The cooperative also specialises in looking after gardens, as well as planted terraces and balconies (see page 220).

An excellent sample of their work is the garden of Scuola Vecchia della Misericordia, a hidden green space of nearly 2500 square metres. The reason it is so remarkable is that it is not only considered a typically Venetian garden, but also a model example of a monastery garden.

The della Misericordia brotherhood moved here in 600, and they used the green space for centuries as a vegetable garden and cemetery.

After the brotherhood was dissolved by Napoleon in 1808, the complex was redesigned as an Italian garden with lawns, trees, shrubs and geometrically laid out flower beds.

In 1920, the artist Italico Brass took over the estate and established his studio here; we have him to thank for the fact that the garden was restored to its original state again, with cypresses, aromatic plants and a "hortus conclusus" (enclosed garden), flower beds and small bux topiary trees.

Address Campo del'Abazia, Cannaregio 3546, 30121 Venice | Opening times Mon – Fri 9am – 12.30am and 2.30 – 5pm | Vaporetto fermata Fondamenta nuove, line B, 4.1/4.2, 5.1/5.2, 12, 13, 22, night route N | Tip Aside from a few rare occasions, a small part of the garden of the Scuola Vecchia della Misericordia is visible through the grate at Rio della Sensa – or by contacting the Wigwam Club Gardini Storici Venezia: www.giardini-venezia.it.

35___ The Valese Art Foundry

Where the sea horses are made

Few people know that metalwork, too, has a long tradition in Venice. One of the foundries still functioning today is the Valese Workshop, with its impressive location next to the church of Madonna dell'Orto, boasting a view of the northern lagoon. Inside, one experiences an atmosphere of a traditional crafts workshop – there is a certain enchantment in its rhythm and rules.

This foundry has been in operation since 1913, and to this day the artisans employ traditional methods using old molds with embossed seals. Many of these molds date back to the 17th and 18th centuries.

The most famous works by Valese are – without a doubt – the trophies for the Venice International Film Festival, which were manufactured here up until the 1950s, as the lions destined for the winners made out of silver and gold steel sheeting were once produced following the designs of the Venetian, Professor Soppelsa. Today, the current trophy – much lighter and made of "mere" gilded or silver-plated brass – is made elsewhere; with funds for the trophies getting ever tighter over the course of the years, the film festival administration decided to save on quality.

However, the famous golden sea horses are still manufactured at Valese, one of the few luxury items that gondolas may be adorned with – even though the vast majority of them are not gilded but consist of polished copper. Some of the greatest artworks are the chandeliers and the ornaments with mythological patterns. And we mustn't forget to mention the metal forms that are produced for the glassmakers of Murano, nor the traditional "musi da porton", the door knockers in the shape of lions' heads with a ring through their nose. All the objects fashioned here are of the finest quality and craftsmanship.

Address Cannaregio Madonna dell'Orto fondamento Gasparo Contarini 3535, 30121 Venice, tel. 0039/41720234 | Opening times Visits by previous appointment, info@valese.it | Vaporetto fermata Orto, line A, 4.1/4.2, 5.1/5.2 | Tip A traditional arts foundry specialising in the manufacture of frames for glass lamps, the Fucina de Rossi workshop, is located not far from the Fondamenta Nuove. And while you're in the area, why not stop at the Ristorante Algiubagio (www.algiubagio.net)?

36_ The Venice Principle
Exhortations carved in stone

There are several spots in Venice where you can find stones that were used for exhortations and notifications – they are entitled "Il Serenissimo Prencipe Fa' Saper". Those plaques proclaimed rules and regulations that usually only pertained to the region where they were placed.

These regulations served to protect residents, to keep the canals and promenades clean, to issue bans on gambling, and to maintain rules of trade and manufacturing.

Of course there was no shortage of threats of semi-draconian punishment; depending on which inquisitor was behind the plaque, they could reach extremes. Here's an example: "… those who infringe upon the divine laws and the honour of the school, will earn as a punishment: flogging, the galley, the pillory and other things, depending on the arbitrary decision of the judges … and a bounty payable to the informer, whose identity will be kept secret, of 200 piccoli from the assets of the accused. For it is the God-fearing and determined will of Our Excellences that this notification be completely obeyed in all its parts. Renegades will be irrevocably punished …" Note that the informers of such deeds were allowed anonymity and even a reward.

Current variations on plaques of this kind with the most varied exhortations can also be found in Venice today, especially around St Mark's Square.

Even though they point in a similar fashion to undesirable activities (ranging from eating ice-cream and making noise to public urination), today's fines are no longer as draconian – a few hundred euros will usually take care of the problem. However, today the money goes exclusively into the municipal coffers, an informer will see nothing of it.

Address Venice Principle Stone (outside the Sotoportego del Magazen – right in front of the Ristorante Al Vagon), Cannaregio 5597, 30131 Venice | Vaporetto fermata Ca' D'oro, line 1, night route N | Tip Another plaque of this kind hangs on the facade facing the Rio dei Mendicanti of the Scuola Grande di San Marco in Castello.

37__The Venus

Explicit advances?

Richard Wagner passed away on 13 February 1883 in the Palazzo Vendramin, as a commemorative plaque on the courtyard wall informs visitors. Though most people today don't come here for Wagner, but to gamble in the Casino.

Those who'd like to avoid bad luck in gambling and hope for luck in love instead, should take a look at the Venus in the courtyard. The unknown beauty draws attention to her femininity with fairly explicit gestures, seemingly wanting to remind us of the sexual escapades that took place behind these walls.

In fact, this palace was the scene of countless romantic entanglements, with the affair of the former owner Abate Vettore Grimani Calergi with actress Anna Maria Santelli going down in history. Nicknamed "Campaspe", this lady was less known for her thespian artistry, than for her qualities as a courtesan. When the cleric noticed that the lady was giving equally free rein to her lovemaking skills in other beds, he flew into a rage of jealousy and had one of his "bravi" (servants, contract killers) shoot her while she was naked on the terrace, recovering from her frivolous exertions, La Campaspe survived albeit with serious injuries. The abbot was sentenced to five years' confinement in a dark cell, but was able to escape with the help of his brothers and go underground.

Richard Wagner, too, was possessed by a passion that kept him on his toes until the very end; an unquenchable sexual desire for a certain Carrie Pringle. Before he died, Wagner was working on a little-known theoretical treatise on eroticism. Allegedly it was after writing the sentence, "At the same time the process of the emancipation of Women only proceeds under ecstatic convulsions. Love – Tragedy", that the quill dropped forever from his hand. The doctor later diagnosed "cardiac arrest caused by ecstasy"!

Address Palazzo Vendramin Calergi, Cannaregio 2040, 30121 Venice | Vaporetto fermata San Marcuola, line 1, night route N | Tip The rooms inhabited by Richard Wagner and his family in the Palazzo Vendramin have been renovated by the Venetian Richard Wagner Society and may be visited.

38___ The Carnival Masks
Tell-tale masks of truth

As most of the masks on sale in Venice today are made in China, locally-produced Venetian masks are a rare find. Here at Stefano Gottardo's, these noble pieces are still made by hand, hiding some of the lost symbolism of the Venetian Carnival, it seems.

The masks, themselves, have their origin in antiquity when the faces of the Gods were covered with masks, to symbolise death and rebirth.

Over the course of history, humankind was constantly torn between a better spiritual life and what were taken to be baser instincts – casually trivialised as the fight between good and evil.

This conflict also forms the background to the Venetian Carnival, channelling the power of evil and making the constant battle between good and evil visible, for a limited timeframe and in a specific context.

It is for this reason that the real Venetian masks are not shrill, colourful and picturesque, but rather ugly, comic and sometimes surreal – after all they were supposed to represent man's darker impulses. Seen in this way, the Venetians are not hiding behind their masks, but rather revealing the true identity of the malign powers that reside within.

In the 18th century, Carnival in Venice lasted several months, making dissolution a fixed part of daily life. The real significance of the festival – which marked the decadence of the time – has been lost.

Since 1978 the Carnival has been focused on tourists. From an artistic point of view, the modern costumes are splendid and a spectacle to behold even if their connection with tradition is rather tenuous.

So today, Carnival in Venice is what it is everywhere: a party!

Address Laboratorio di artigianato artistico, Calle Lunga S.Maria Formosa, Castello 5174/b, 30122 Venice, tel. 0039/415229995, papiermache@papiermache.it | **Vaporetto fermata** Ospedale, line B, 4.1/4.2, 5.1/5.2, 22 | **Tip** A real Carnival costume is not complete without the three-cornered hat and a (preferably black) cape. You'll find everything you need in the seemingly endless range of historical and modern costumes on offer at Stefano's, costume designer and make-up artist – for rent and for sale; however, these gems can easily set you back 4000 euros and more, depending on the level of detail (www.nicolao.com).

39__The Cathedra Petri

Mysterious bishop's seat

The old name for the island of San Pietro di Castello with its eponymous basilica was "Isola Olivolo", as it is the shape of an olive and it
is said that olives were, in fact, once cultivated here. The island was
among the first to be settled in Venice. In 1451 San Pietro di Castello became the seat of the Patriarch of Venice, until it was outstripped
by San Marco under Napoleon. For many centuries San Pietro was
the centre of the Venetian clergy.

Today, hardly anyone visits here, even though there would be a
compelling reason for doing so: the Cathedra Petri, the legendary
bishop's seat of Saint Peter, which is shrouded in mystery. According to legend, Peter the Apostle founded the eponymous patriarchate
in Antiochia (today's Antakya in Turkey) in 34 AD, and this cathedra was supposedly his bishop's seat – moreover, crusaders are said to
have hidden the Holy Grail inside.

What is truly interesting about this seat and a mystery that has
remained unsolved to this day, is its backrest. The fact that the backrest is adorned with Arabic letters from the Koran and a six-point-
ed star suggest it is a 13th-century Muslim sepulchral stele, which
would be rather unusual, to say the least, for a bishop's seat.

Stigmatised since the Jewish persecutions, the hexagram originally appears in Christianity and even in Islam. What is probably
widely unknown amongst both Jews and Muslims is that this star,
called "Seal of Solomon" was a seal serving to banish evil spirits and
demons – in both Jewish as well as Arabic cultures – and, due to its
shape, was in fact a symbol for dual harmony.

Though perhaps it is irrelevant as to what is fact and what is fiction here. Wouldn't it be much more meangingful to see the Cathedra as a symbol of harmony and peace?

Address Basilica San Pietro di Castello (the Cathedra is located on to the right of the entrance), Campo San Pietro, island of San Pietro di Castello 2787, 30122 Venice, tel. 0039/412750462 | Opening times Mon–Sat 10am–5pm | Vaporetto fermata San Pietro, line 4.1/4.2 and 5.1/5.2 | Tip Across from the island, on Campo Ruga, you'll find the city's lowest "sotoportego" (footpath under a building). A nearby house in Campazzo de l'Erba 394 is very interesting too, showing an unusual architectural feature: the various adjacent flats are connected by an exterior balcony – in the 19th century this served to unite the living and working areas, increasing efficiency and giving the workers the opportunity to benefit from more flexible working hours.

40__Cicchetti

The incarnation of the sardine

"Cicchetti" is the name for the typical snacks and small dishes served in Venetian bars. Similar to Spanish tapas, these specialties are enjoyed in small portions, with a glass of ombra (see page 170), an aperitivo or a glass of beer. The fish, seafood or vegetables are usually deep-fried, grilled or cooked and offered up as finger food, with toothpicks or on little skewers. Small panini or sandwiches can also count as a cicchetto.

Venetians partake of their cicchetti almost exclusively in the morning or as a snack accompanying alcoholic drinks – rarely as a proper meal.

Alongside the "baccalà mantecato" (see page 104), the "sarde in saòr" are maybe the best cicchetto there is, and for many gourmets the very incarnation of the sardine. Saòr is the Venetian term for "sapore", meaning enjoyment, taste or spice – and the cicchetto that emphatically ticks all those boxes is the "sarde in saòr".

The origins of this dish go back to Venice's seafaring tradition. The saòr – a marinade of vinegar, oil, onions and sometimes herbs – was used by sailors to preserve fish and seafood, which provided them with a lasting supply of protein and vitamins on their voyages. And it is a fact that Venetian sailors and seafarers never suffered from scurvy.

The method of preservation was originally developed in the Arab world, probably in Persia. It then reached the lagoon city via Byzance, as Venice was part of the Byzantine Empire for many centuries.

And following an old Byzantine custom, the sarde in saòr – in the cold season in particular – are refined with raisins and pine nuts, which doesn't only lend them their typical sweet-and-sour aroma, but turns the popular dish into a true delicacy. Other versions of the dish sometimes include cinnamon or thin slices of lemon.

Address Bacarando ai Corazzieri, Salizada del Pignater, Castello 3839, 30100 Venice, tel. 0039/415289859 | Opening times Daily 10.30am–midnight | Vaporetto fermata Arsenale, line B, 1, 4.1/4.2 | Tip An excellent range of cicchetti (including delicacies such as nervetti, tripe, spleen, musetto, snails and the like) is on offer at the Cicchetteria attached to the Ristorante Da Fiore (Calle delle Botthege). Those who like a cosy and authentic environment should head for Rialto and the Cantina do Mori (San Polo 429), the Do Spade (http://cantinadospade.com) or the Osteria al Diavolo e l'Acquasanta (San Polo 561/B).

41__ The Colleoni Monument

Meeting point for lovers

"As early as seven o'clock I took up position at the monument to the hero, Colleoni. At exactly eight o'clock, I saw a double-oared gondola dock, and a masked shape emerge. Without exchanging a single word, we headed for St Mark's Square and entered the house, which was only a hundred paces from the San Moisè theatre", wrote Casanova in his memoirs. So, the meeting point for these secret trysts with his lover, a nun from Murano (see page 20), was the Colleonio Monument. Colleonio was the incarnation of the Renaissance "condottiere", a political and military adventurer whose spirit couldn't be broken by a bad spell in the dungeon or the turmoil of war.

Casanova, however wasted no time admiring the conqueror of Terraferma (the name for the areas to the east of northern Italy, subjugated by Venice from the 15th century onwards). His mind was already in the Casino and with Aretino's Ex Libris (see page 190): "I have here a little book, which was in the position of Pietro Aretino. Over the next three hours I'd like to try exploring these."

The position of the equestrian statue of Colleoni, in the Campo outside the Chiesa Santi Giovanni e Paolo, called Zanipolo for short in Venetian, is not a coincidence. Colleoni had named the city of Venice as his heir, with the condition, however, that he would in turn receive a monument in front of San Marco. While the Venetians, adverse to any kind of personality cult, didn't really like this idea, and they didn't want to renounce a substantial fortune either. Clever "avvocati" (lawyers) came up with a cunning solution, interpreting the testamentary stipulation in such a way that the condottiere couldn't have been referring to the basilica of San Marco, but rather the Scuola di San Marco, the confraternity next to Zanipolo. In this way the statue was erected at the location where it still stands today, "in compliance with stipulations", and the city was able to access its "legitimate" inheritance.

Address Campo Santi Giovanni e Paolo, Castello, 30122 Venice | Vaporetto fermata
Ospedale, line B, 4.1/4.2, 5.1/5.2, 22 | Tip The equestrian statue of Bartolomeo Colleoni
was made in a foundry near the Palazzo Rizzo-Patarol. Today's Corte Cavallo owes its
name to that horse. In the Palazzo Rizzo-Patarol (today the Hotel dei Doge) a historic
ice cellar hides beneath the planted hill.

42 The Garnier Elephant

Lethal church visit

A great way of unearthing Venetian curiosities is by searching the extensive city archives. One of the most remarkable events of this kind occurred during the Carnival season 1818/19.

During the course of the general fun and games, one of the animals known as a Garnier elephant, was brought into the Serenissima.

Another of the numerous carnivalesque attractions was a fleet firing such piercing salvoes that they not only caused substantial damage to facades and chimneys, but also, to make matters worse, enraged the elephant bull to the point that he destroyed his menagerie, wreaking terrible havoc.

While attempts to lock the animal in a warehouse were successful, a warden trying to calm the elephant down with food was trampled to death.

Finally the elephant managed to escape once more, running in the direction of Ca' di Dio, where he gobbled refreshments at a fruit stall. After that he turned towards the Calle del Dose, trotted across the Campo della Bragora, to finally end up in the church of Sant'Antonin. All this happened amongst useless volleys of gunfire by the irate Venetians. None of this, however, did anything to harm the pachyderm.

Unfortunately, the elephant ensconced in the church did not find the hoped-for celestial assistance. The Venetians bore a large hole through the wall and took aim at the animal twice with a cannon, making it collapse, lethally wounded, in "un lago di sangue" (a pool of blood). In a further display of their commercial nous, the Venetians didn't just bury the cadaver, but sold it, for 800 florins, to the natural history section of the University of Padua, where it spent a hundred years, taxidermied, until it was of, eaten by moths.

Address Church of Sant'Antonin, Campo Sant'Antonin, Castello, 30122 Venice. As the church Sant'Antonin isn't really a sight in its own right, we've selected a photo of a rare representation of an arch angel (probably Michael or Raphael) with an elephant. It stands in a courtyard of the new Procuratie (funnily enough on the way to the First Aid station.) | Vaporetto fermata Aresenale, line B, 1, 4.1/4.2 | Tip Also interesting is the rhinoceros mosaic in St Mark's, another reminder of a lethal show – however, the rhinoceros wasn't killed but died during the crossing in a sea storm.

43___The Marble Tile

Tools telling workers' history

In the church of San Martino you'll see the various tools used by ship-yard workers engraved on a tile on the floor. Why? The caulkers had an altar here (the second on the right).

The caulkers and the tarriers shared responsibility for sealing the space between ships' planks: first flax tow (cheap fibres made from processing hemp and flax) was hammered into the seams of the hull, using caulking irons and hammers, which were then sealed with tar.

Both groups of workers enjoyed certain privileges, such as being exempt from military service, and were allowed to earn money on the side working privately on commercial ships.

Strolling down the Via Garibaldi, a closer look at the window display of number 1791 reveals old tools and model ships. This was the seat of the Società di Mutuo Soccorso fra Carpentieri e Calafati, the Mutual Aid Society of Carpenters and Caulk Workers.

Inside, they keep tools and items belonging to the shipyard work-ers. The most valuable piece is likely the "Mariegola", the register and statutes of this traditional organisation, probably the oldest of its kind in Venice.

Founded in 1867, it was something like a workers' cooperative for carpenters and caulkers, whose members paid into a fund used to provide health insurance.

Today, the association is open to all Venetian citizens, with health insurance based on the monies available through annual contribu-tions by its members. Craftsmen from varied professions – particu-lary those threatened by obsolescence – are members of this com-munity, which makes them more or less the preservers of these old trades.

Address Church of San Martino, Campo die San Martino, Castello 2298c, 30122 Venice, tel. 0039/415230487 | **Opening times** Mon–Sat 8.45–11.45am and 4.30–7.30pm, Sun 8am–12 noon; the cooperative may be visited only by previous appointment by emailing smscc@smscc.it) | **Vaporetto fermata** Arsenale, line 1, 4.1/4.2, night route N | **Tip** The shipyard workers formed a kind of elite amongst the craftsmen and were proud to be able to serve the seafaring nation and sea power that was Venice; they also enjoyed various privileges, such as free accommodation near the Arsenale. You can still see remnants of the old workers' flats in Rio delle Gorne at the Fondamenta dei Penini – an inscription between nos. 2445 and 2446 points to a "seghe" (saw master) and "calafati" (caulking workers).

44 Maria Lactans

Illustrated breastfeeding

Venice was once a stronghold for artistic representations of what is known to art historians as Maria lactans, the breastfeeding Mother of God. For centuries it was perfectly natural to represent a breastfeeding woman.

This particular motif was already common in ancient Egypt, where the goddess Isis gives her breast to the boy Horus, a symbol of fertility. The image of a Maria lactans emerged in the Byzantine Empire around the 14th century, yet with a different meaning: here, the child represents God, connecting with humankind through the mother's breast – from this angle, the act of breastfeeding can also be seen as a sign of Christ's humanity.

Representations of the Maria lactans were a typical theme in the Middle Ages, and taken up by the Cistercians, in particular. Christianity interpreted the symbolism of the motherly breast as a sign of mercy; some images show what was known as the Virgin of Mercy, who – in order to divert God's anger from humankind – points to her uncovered breast, used to feed Christ. This kind of symbolism was sometimes used for pilgrimage sites as miraculous images for "women's concerns".

Here, the breastfeeding woman doesn't always have to be the Virgin Mary; some artists represented the motif as a symbol for maternity in general. Later representations, in the 19th and 20th centuries – regardless of whether they showed Mary and Jesus, or simply mother and child – have a strongly iconographic character and in modern times have been used by advocates of breastfeeding. A fairly unknown yet well-preserved Maria lactans can be found in a dark side chapel of San Francesco della Vigna – unfortunately this remarkable work of art is often overlooked, as you first have to feed a coin into a machine in order to illuminate it.

Address San Francesco della Vigna, Ramo al Ponte San Francesco della Vigna, Castello, 30122 Venice | Vaporetto fermata Celestia, line 4.1/4.2, 5.1/5.2 | Tip The famous painting "The Tempest" by Giorgione, which hangs in the Gallerie dell'Accademia, also represents a breastfeeding woman – in this case, however, nearly naked. The painting is a typical example of Venetian painting, which emphasised moods, and it is an image full of the secrets, awaiting discovery in a sensual-erotic world.

45 _ Pompeo Giustiniani

A one-armed hero

Many Doges, military commanders and notables of Venice have found their last resting place, or are honoured in some way or another, in the basilica of San Giovanni e Paolo, Zanipolo for short. One of them is a certain Pompeo Giustiniani, who might not be buried here yet whose magnificent equestrian monument adorns one side of the church nave. This, in itself, would not be noteworthy, yet a closer look reveals an interesting detail: Giustiniani's statue is missing its right arm. Why? The artwork is not damaged, nor is it a case of a stonemason's slapdash work.

Pompeo Giustiniani was born in 1560 in Ajaccio on Corsica, in the same city, by the way, as Napoleon Bonaparte a few centuries later. Starting his military career at only 14 years of age, in the service of Genova, he changed allegiance to the Spaniards until he received the office of commander in Venice.

At the siege of Ostende – which is remembered in world history books for the high loss of life on both sides as "the long Carnival of Death" – he fought on the side of the Spanish. In the melée a bullet tore apart his right arm, which had to be amputated and replaced with a metal prosthetic. From then on he acquired the nickname, "braccio di ferro" (iron arm).

In 1613 he entered service in Venice, leading the Venetian troops in the war against the Uskokes, a group of Hajdukes, consisting mainly of Croatian, but also of Serbian refugees who'd fled from the Ottomans and had declared war on both the Ottomans and Venice.

On 11 October, 1617, Giustiniani lost his life in the battle of Gradisca, hit by a lethal Habsburgian bullet.

The equestrian statue erected in his honour only shows his left side, to cover up the missing arm.

Address Basilica San Giovanni e Paolo, Campo San Giovanni e Paolo, Castello 6363, 30122 Venice | **Opening times** Mon–Sat 7.30am–6.30pm, Sun 12 noon–7.30pm | **Vaporetto fermata** Ospedale, line B, 4.1/4.2, 5.1/5.2, 22 | **Tip** Right past the entrance of the basilica there is an interesting fresco. It represents the Ottomans skinning the Venetian governor of Cyprus, Marcantonio Bragadin, after the fall of Nikosia in 1571. Stuffed with straw, the macabre trophy was taken to Constantinople, where it was stolen in 1580 by the Venetian, Gerolamo Polidori, and taken back to Venice. Today, the skin is kept as a relic in the church, without accessibility to the public, however.

46__ The Red Stone

The miracle of Corte Nova

The Sotoportego in Corte Nova has been the scene of many a strange happening. In the lunette, above the entrance, visitors may read of the miracles that occured thanks to the intercession of the Virgin Mary.

According to legend, the residents of the estate were spared from death several times due to their strong faith and were even spared a great epidemic. While the terrible plague of 1630 claimed over 50,000 victims in Venice alone, Giovanna, a young girl from Corte Nova, pleaded with the members of her family, her friends and her neighbours not to give up hope and to put their faith in the help of the Mother of God. She painted an image of the Virgin Mary, Saint Roque (patron saint of plague victims) and Saint Lorenzo Giustiniani (patron saint protecting against epidemics), and hung this in the Sotoportego.

All residents of the area were now called to prayer each day in front of this image and, sure enough, the plague, which was to claim countless more victims, didn't spread into the vicinity, sparing all of Giovanna's neighbours. To commemorate this event, a red cobblestone of Veronese marble was set into the ground.

Following this miraculous event, the Mother of God was also invoked here during the First World War, and it appears as if the residents' strong faith worked once again as a protective shield, this time against the bombardments, as there were no victims in Venice.

Still today, the rosary is said in the Sotoportego on the first Tuesday in May and on 21 November – the day of the Madonna della Salute, commemorating the end of the plague epidemic of 1638. Many people also step on that red stone, meant to bring good luck – others consider this heresy, as it's well known that you shouldn't tempt fate!

Address Sotoportego Corte Nova (near Calle Zorzi, not far from Santa Giustina), Castello 6318, 30122 Venice | **Vaporetto fermata** Arsenale, line 1, 4.1/4.2, night route N | **Tip** Not far from the Sotoportego at Castello 3253, the Palazzo Malta is the seat of the Great Priory of the Maltese Order in Venice, which may be visited by prior appointment (www.ordinedimaltaitalia.org).

47__ The Revolving Door
Unwanted children

In Calle della Pietà, where the eponymous convent once stood, two remnants serve as a reminder that there was a hatch here, where one could abandon "unwanted children – with a quiet conscience". Yet you were exhorted to do this only in the case of extreme hardship.

The unusual sign hanging on the side wall of today's della Pietà church proclaims that parents with sufficient funds to raise their offspring themselves are strictly prohibited from abandoning children. According to the threat on this plaque, those not following this order were to be "damned and excommunicated". This papal bull issued by Pope Paul III on 12 November 1548, used to hang on the other side of the street – and with good reason.

Opposite, at the start of Calle della Pietà, you can make out a small revolving door which now belongs to the Hotel Metropole. In the past, this "revolving door of the innocent" as it was known, was a kind of "baby hatch", though only parts of the original construction still remain.

Pope Innocenz III (1160–1216) institutionalised this practice of formal baby hatches, whereupon "revolving doors of the innocent" were created all over Europe. This allowed parents who saw no other option to hand over their children anonymously. The doors consisted of a cradle accessible from outside that the child could be placed in. The sound of a bell alerted the nuns who would turn the door and take the baby into the care of the convent. The outside also had a grid with an aperture only large enough to hand a baby through.

While this kind of foundling wheel was discontinued over the course of the 19th century, they are once again in use nearly everywhere in Europe, due to an ever-rising number of abandoned babies since the end of the last century.

Address Calle della Pietà, Castello, 30122 Venice (the revolving door is located to the right, at the Hotel Metropole, the plaque to the left on the wall of the church of della Pietà) | Vaporetto fermata San Zaccaria, line B, 1, 2, 4.1/4.2, 5.1/5.2, 14, 15, 19, 20, night route N | Tip The church of La Pietà has the peculiarity of having been designed as a concert hall, because in the past young orphan girls from the convent would perform here – today you can still see the cast-iron grids on the two lateral walls of the church where the girls used to sit. Contrary to the often-repeated legends, Vivaldi never performed here, as today's church wasn't even built when he died. He did play in the former church, della Pietà, of which only two pillars have been preserved, which can be seen to the right, at the end of the Hotel Metropole lobby.

48_ The Runes
A tast of north in Venice

Four lions guard the gate to the Arsenal. One of the two lions on the left bears strange letters. For a long time nothing was known about their meaning, until the Danish historian, Carl Christian Rafn, recognised them as runes, dating from the 11th century, which had been inscribed there by the order of Harald III (1015 – 1066), telling of his deeds in Greece, Romania and Armenia – as a kind of evidence of "having been there". The lion arrived in the city as part of the war booty of Doge Francesco Morosini (who entered the annals of history for hitting Athen's Acropolis with gunfire by mistake, sending the edifice, used as an ammunition depot, up in the air).

What is interesting in the context of the runes is the Venetian recipe for "baccalà mantecato" (codfish puree). According to legend, codfish arrived in Venice in the 15th century by means of the merchant, Piero Querini, who became familiar with the dried stockfish on a journey (blown off course, in truth) to the Lofotes. For the Venetians, the fish sounded like the Portuguese "bacalhau", which settled its name.

Another probability is that the Venetians already knew the Portuguese version of the codfish, namely the klipfish, which would also explain the famous codfish cream used to prepare mascarpone. In contrast to Norwegian codfish, klipfish is heavily salted, which the Venetians would have tried to tone down with the mascarpone.

Venetians, who tend to use very little salt, seem to have taken more to the unsalted Norwegian product: the logo of the "Dogale Confraternita del Baccalà Mantecato" (Confraternity of Codfish Puree) features a Norwegian fisherman alongside dried fish and promotes a puree where the soaked and boiled codfish is only prepared with olive oil (without the mascarpone).

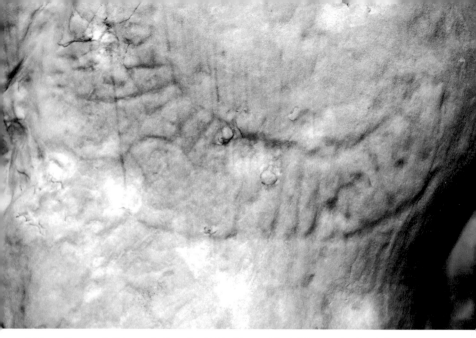

Address Campo de l'Arsenal, Castello, 30122 Venice (the left lion at the front) | **Vaporetto fermata** Arsenale, line 1, 4.1/4.2, night route N | **Tip** In front of the Latteria Ortiz in Castello you can usually see a large wooden barrel with pre-soaked codfish for domestic use. The Norwegians export two-thirds of their codfish production to Italy, with the Venetians consuming 50 per cent of it, but only the unsalted variety; the salted klipfish is sold in the rest of Italy. It is interesting how a former seafarer's food and later fasting fare was able to rise to become a highly acclaimed delicacy.

49__ The Sala San Marco
The "bloody" library

This is certainly one of those hidden places of Venice that not even the locals really know about, the mysterious hall that goes by the name of Sala San Marco Biblioteca. This was the assembly room of the former San Marco confraternity; today, the building is used as a hospital.

The library of San Marco is situated in the chapter house on the first floor. The centre of the nearly completely gilded wooden ceiling is adorned with a golden Venetian lion and an open book. It is surrounded by the symbols of the other great "scuole" (confraternities); the eagle representing San Giovanni Evangelista, the cross with the concentric circles for the Carità, the abbreviation SR for San Rocco (see page 210) and SM for Santa Maria di Valverde. Thus the Scuola not only served for meditation purposes, but also for interaction with other confraternities and mutual assistance. The four famous paintings by Domenico Tintoretto that used to adorn the walls, fell victim to Napoleon's plundering – three of which however were eventually returned to Venice and today hang in the Academy. In 1806 the Scuola was converted into barracks, after that into a military hospital and then in 1819 into a civilian hospital with 120 beds. The building was restored in 1948.

Since 1985 the library has been home to a permanent exhibition entitled "The History of Health – Venice and the Hospital from the 16th to the 20th Century". The exhibition contains important documents from the old library, anatomy atlases and also plans for redesigning the hospital.

The core of the exhibition, however, is the large collection of surgical instruments, ranging from simple bone saws for the amputation of all of limbs to bizarre utensils for skull surgery – truly a bloody place!

Address Campo Santi Giovanni e Paolo, Castello, 30122 Venice | Opening times
Mon–Fri 8.30am–2pm (except public holidays, Assumption Day and 24 Dec–1 Jan) |
Vaporetto fermata Ospedale, line B, 4.1/4.2, 5.1/5.2, 22 | Tip The nearby Barbaria delle
Tole in the house with the no. 6671 shelters the cosy Trattoria Bandierette.

50__The Secret Message

A politically motivated bridge railing

"Risorgimento" (renaissance) is a term used by the Italians, both for the historical era between 1815 and 1870, and for the political movements working towards an independent nation state of Italy following the 1814/1815 Congress of Vienna. The Congress of Vienna left the kingdom of Sardinia as the last independent Italian state. Against a background of a desire for national unity (brought about by the continuing removal of the political changes by Napoleon), the year of 1848, in particular, saw revolts against foreign rule – with the kingdom of Sardinia taking on a leading role, as it still had an indigenous dynasty.

In 1848, the first attack on Austrian-dominated Lombard-Veneto took place, under the leadership of King Emanuel II of Sardinia; the uprising was quelled however.

In 1861, following further revolutionary uprisings and the Italian Wars of Independence, the kingdom of Italy was finally able to claim its new identity as a constitutional monarchy, dominated by the kingdom of Sardinia; 17 March, 1861, saw the proclamation of the king of Sardinia, Victor Emanuel II, as King of Italy.

Venice, for its part, initially stayed under Austrian rule (see page 224) and was only added to the new Italian kingdom following the Austrian defeat at the hands of Prussia in the Austro-Prussian War in 1866.

At the time of Austrian rule, political activism and voicing criticism was dangerous; the city was swarming with Austrian secret police agents. Which is why people resorted to secret and coded messages – such as the ones found on a bridge railing; at first glance the cast-iron shapes appear to be hearts, yet a closer look reveals the letters "W V E", standing for "Viva Vittorio Emanuele" (Long Live Vittorio Emanuele).

Address Ponte de Borgoloco, Calle Borgolocco, Castello, 30122 Venice | Vaporetto fermata Ospedale, line B, 4.1/4.2, 5.1/5.2, 22 | Tip The Borgoloco located behind the bridge takes its name from the Venetian phrase "tegnir uno a loco e foco", which roughly translates as giving somebody shelter. The Borgoloco then was a part of town with numerous guest rooms and inns.

51__The Storeroom

Did Saint Mark have a vision here?

The small "Cappella della Visione di San Marco" (Chapel of the Vision of Saint Mark), today used as a storeroom, is the place where, according to legend, Saint Mark was surprised by a tempest on his way back from (or on his way to, depending on the version) Aquileia, and had to seek shelter.

An angel came and said: "Peace be with you, Mark, my Evangelist." The "pax tibi Marce Evangelista meus" was adopted by Venice in various ways. The angel continued: "Don't be afraid, you still have a lot to suffer. After your death a city will be established here where your body will find eternal rest, and you will become its patron saint." Back in Rome, Mark told his teacher, Peter, about this vision, asking him to make Hermagora bishop of Aquileia, as he had witnessed in his vision.

The vision is a milestone in the history of the legendary foundation of the city of Venice, serving the Venetians in securing their political and religious dominance over Aquileia and Grado.

In 828, to consolidate its position, Venice stole the mortal remains of Saint Mark from Alexandria. The relics proved to be of great significance, allowing Venice to emancipate itself from the dominance of the Roman emperors and to force through the independence of its church.

The true background, however, was the fight over jurisdiction; in 827 – only one year before the emergence of the legend and the stealing of the relics – Aquileia had been "awarded" the remains, arguing that Saint Mark had, after all, preached in Aquileia. With the legend of the vision – in particular, the version claiming that Saint Mark had been travelling to, rather than from Aquiliea, meaning he hadn't yet been preaching there – and the stealing of the relics, the balance of power shifted to benefit Venice.

Address Courtyard of the "Patronate" of the church of San Francesco della Vigna, Campo San Francesco della Vigna, Castello 2786, 30122 Venice, tel. 0039/415206102 | Opening times Visits during church opening times by request, daily 8am–12.30 and 3–6pm | Vaporetto fermata Celestia, line 4.1/4.2 und 5.1/5.2 | Tip The monastery of San Francesco della Vigna also boasts an extraordinary vegetable garden-cum-vineyard; it is the very vines that gave the monastery its name ("vigna" = vine). The gardens are accessible to the public during opening times (daily 8am–12 noon and 3–7pm) if you ask nicely.

52__ The Used Clothes Collection

Second-hand in holy walls

Venice Old Town has no flea markets in the usual sense of the term – where mainly private individuals offer a mixed bag of unwanted objects, books, clothing or other everyday items – yet here, too, there is an exception to the rule in the shape of one such market held in Cannaregio, near the church of Santa Maria dei Miracoli on the Campo Santa Marian Nova (a popular flea market, by the way, which merits attention). Apart from this exception, most markets are actually more or less antique fairs, with predominantly professional vendors, and these are usually organised by the city of Venice. For instance in Castello you have the Mercatino delle Robe da Mar, which, as the name indicates, sells mainly objects for seafaring, sailing or fishery, or the slightly mournful-sounding Mercatino Polvere di Ricordi, which roughly translates as "Market of the Dust of Memory" – the objects on offer certainly fit this description.

Those trying to get rid of old clothing or other everyday items who don't want to wait around for one of the rare opportunities for selling at a regular flea market, do have an alternative – found in the Chiesa di San Martino building. By the way, while the cult of Saint Martin is much celebrated around this parish, it has much less significance in Venice than in other European countries, such as Austria or Germany. What is interesting here is the door to the right of the main entrance; take a look inside and you might be tempted to think that there's a flea market going on. And, in fact, it is something similar: a kind of second-hand shop, for selling clothing that no longer fits, unneeded everyday items, and second-hand books. The proceeds go to charity.

Address Chiesa di San Martino, Campo S. Martin (Fondamenta di Fronte), Castello 2298, 30122 Venezia | Opening times Mon–Sat 8.45–11.45am and 4.30–7.30pm, Sun 8am–12 noon | Vaporetto fermata Arsenale, line B, 1, 4.1/4.2 | Tip Between May and Christmas the Santa Reparata chapel in the church of Santi Geremia e Lucia, in the Cannaregio neighbourhood, turns into a small shop for real Murano glass (open 10am–2pm and 4–7pm); a curiosity off the beaten tourist track that's well worth seeing.

53_ The White Stone
Meeting point of the great

On the cobblestoned path leading to San Pietro di Castello (see page 86), a conspicuously white stone catches the eye amongst the regular grey of the cobbles. Now you might think that it lies here through mere coincidence, but this is not the case. On the contrary, the white stone marks a location of great significance for the history of the Serenissima. It was exactly here, at this spot of the Campo San Pietro, that the Doge and the Patriarch of Venice would meet.

Few people remember that up until 1807 the church of San Pietro di Castello was the cathedral church of Venice, not St Mark's Basilica; the latter served as a private chapel to the Doges and was not accessible to the public. This created a dilemma for both the Patriarch and the Doge: neither wanted to go to the other's church service, which both saw as a humiliation.

Now how to both spare the Doge the embarrassment of having to come all the way to the church of San Pietro, and avoid the Patriarch having to receive the Doge on arrival by boat or, even worse, appear at an audience in the Doge's palace? A diplomatic maneuver was used which upheld the honour of both parties equally by way of an ingenious compromise: it was agreed that the Doge and the Patriarch would meet at the precise spot which today is marked by this white stone.

Incidentally, we have Napoleon to thank for the fact that the Basilica of San Marco was made the cathedral of Venice. At the basis for this decision was a certain political consideration. Now that San Marco was the cathedral church, the Doges were deprived of their private chapel, which meant losing one of the most important symbols of their power. Thus Napoleon was able to weaken their influence even before arriving in the Serenissima.

Address Campo San Pietro, Castello, 30122 Venice | **Vaporetto fermata** San Pietro, line 4.1/4.2 and 5.1/5.2 | **Tip** Behind the church of San Pietro, you'll find the former palace of the Patriarch; going through the cloisters here you'll be able to make out, at the farther end, a dark corridor with a gate. That gate leads to the small Elio de Pellegrini shipyard, which is open to the public on weekdays (simply ring the doorbell; www.cantieredepellegrini.it).

54__ The Boccia Lane

Beach fun in the city

Venice always has a surprise up its sleeve – particulary when it comes to the gambling, entertainment and tourism industries. In this case the Serenissima presents a highly amusing surprise, yet in an unusually modest and retiring way. The area near the church of Angelo Raffaele hides not one, but two boccia clubs: Mariano Cucco's (Dorsoduro 2531 in the Fondamenta Briati) on the one hand, and San Sebastiano on the other.

In more northerly climes, boccia tends to be known as a beach game or perhaps for being the favourite sport of German Chancellor, Konrad Adenauer. In Italy, boccia has remained a sport of the people to this day, and is by no means only played on the beach, but in sports halls created for this purpose.

Members of the Boccia Club of San Sebastiano have three regulation lanes at their disposal, with beginners, amateur players and professionals taking turns to train for competitions or simply getting a game in.

When no competitions are on, guests are more than welcome too; they may either order an ombra at the osteria and watch, or have a go themselves. However, this is only really recommended for those with experience, given the fact that the players pitching their skills against each other here tend to have a certain level of training.

The reason boccia became such a popular sport in Italy is because it was the favourite hobby of Giuseppe Garibaldi. The sport had its heyday in 1940s Italy and in the post-war era, which saw a veritable boom.

When the game mutated from a hobby to a serious sport, associations were founded in order to provide players with professional training opportunities.

Address Boccia Club San Sebastiano, Fondamenta San Sebastiano, Dorsoduro 2371, 30123 Venice | **Opening times** Mon–Sat 10am–12.30pm and 3.30–7pm | **Vaporetto fermata** San Basilio, line 2, 5.1/5.2, 8, night route N | **Tip** Those interested in Venice's only city-centre tennis court should head for the Ca' San Boldo, Rio Terà I, San Polo 2281 – anybody can play a round of tennis here; surely a treat, and not restricted to guests of the holiday apartments (for bookings email info@adriabella.com).

55___The Do Farai

Venetian sashimi

In the Osteria Do Farai – the establishment, by the way, where the victory festivities following the great regatta are held each year – you'll find a fabulously tasty delicacy on the menu, "Carpaccio di Branzino Ubriaco di Prosecco".

This is freshly caught sea bass is filleted in front of the guest and marinated in prosecco – and though "ubriaco" means "drunk," the most you'll feel from the small amount of alcohol used in the dish is "brillo" (tipsy).

What is admirable here is that the fish is not filleted with finely sharpened Japanese knives as you might think, but with the aid of a meat fork and a butcher's knife. The fact that the fish still ends up in paper-thin slices on the platter proves that a trade learned well is still more important than any tools.

As you enjoy this delicacy, rustic as it is elegant, you can't help noticing the freshness of the fish, which, especially with raw fish, is a must. What is interesting in this context is that the first floor of the building of the Pescheria Nuova (New Fish Market) used to house the state prosecutor's office, whose rooms could be accessed by a flight of steps decorated with shells, octopus and fish heads. One of the cast-iron gates under the stairs bears the inscription "Piscis primum a capite foetet", which, translated from the Greek by Erasmus of Rotterdam, means "The fish starts stinking from the head".

The question is: who was the saying referring to? It could hardly have been the fish vendors, as they would have been aware of this particular fact. Nor the buyers probably, as Venetians would have known their way around the wares. Thus the "stinking head" must have been a warning allusion to the municipal civil servants working here and their high positions of power.

Address Osteria Do Farai, Dorsoduro 3278, 30123 Venice, tel. 0039/412770369 | **Opening times** Mon–Sat 11.30am–2.30pm and 7–10.45pm | **Vaporetto fermata** Ca' Rezzonico, line A, 1 | **Tip** Behind the Pescheria Nuova in the direction of Canal Grande you'll discover a plaque stipulating the exact times for fishing and measurements – these rules had to be followed to the letter. This measure was an early attempt to guarantee the quality of the fish and a sustainable fishing industry within the lagoon.

56__ The Dog Relief
Symbol of the "Padri dell'acquavita"

At Rio Terà dei Gesuati there is a keystone featuring a relief of a dog and a shield. The latter shows a star and a torch, which together form a lily.

All these attributes point to the order of the Jesuates – not to be confused with the Jesuits – and can be explained as follows: the mother of Saint Dominic once dreamed about a dog bearing a torch in its mouth, in her opinion a sign that her child would set the world on fire with his words and thus change it. The dog also points to the literal translation of the name Dominikus (Domenico in Italian), which can combine two parts: "domini" (Master) and "cane" (dog). In fact, the origin of the name is "domenica", the Italian word for Sunday – the mother chose it in memory of the pilgrimage she undertook shortly before giving birth to Saint Dominikus of Silos.

The star symbolises wisdom, on the one hand, on the other it's a reminder of the fact that on the birthday of Saint Dominic a star lit up the sky. The lily is the symbol of faith, wisdom and courage, but can also be interpreted as a symbol of chastity – this was a criticism on the part of the Jesuates of the clergy, mired in in sexual scandals under Pope John XXII (1316–1334).

The Jesuates aimed to achieve salvation of the soul through prayer, self-castigation, charitable good works and looking after the sick – becoming famous, most of all, for taking care of plague victims. The people lovingly called them "Padri dell'acquavita" (Aquavites), as they would administer many tasty healing liqueurs to their patients. Even so, in 1668 the order was dissolved by Clemens IX at the urgent behest of the city of Venice, the Lion City needing the wealth of the order for the continuation of their war against the Turks.

Address Rio Terà dei Gesuati, Dorsoduro, 30123 Venice | Vaporetto fermata Zattere, line B, 2, 5.1/5.2, 6, 8, 10, 16, night route N | Tip The dei Gesuati church features a glass door with the inscription "Don Orione Artigianelli", "artigianelli" meaning something related to craftsmen; this is a reference to the fact that it was important to Don Orione that the adolescents he supported learn a trade. The building is a former convent; its fine cloisters have been preserved and may be visited by prior appointment (info@donorione-venezia.it).

57__ The Faded Coat of Arms
Veronica Franco's birthplace

Above the parish offices of the Chiesa di Sant'Agnese, you can make out a strange emblem, its coat-of-arms is nearly completely faded. This, you see, is the coat of arms of the Franco family, one member of which was the most famous courtesan in Venice, the mythical Veronica Franco – and this is her place of birth. It is by no means a coincidence that the coat of arms was placed at the Parrocchia, as the Francos were what were called "cittadini originari" ("original" Venetians). As such, they were intrinsically linked to their neighbourhood and neighbours, who used this symbol to express their gratitude and recognition of the family.

Veronica learned the art of love early on from her mother, who was a "cortigiana onesta", or intellectual courtesan. Veronica, too, was listed in 1565 in the "Catalogo Pi ù honorate cortigiane Di Venezia" (see page 180), the catalogue of elite courtesans. These women were educated, attractive and enjoyed a good reputation; they were allowed to sit for famous painters and even to enter churches. As one of them, Veronica's left nipple would become world famous due to Jacopo Tintoretto's sensual-erotic partial nude painting of her. Veronica studied philosophy and counted poets and painters amongst her friends, patrons and lovers. 1575 saw the publication of her love poetry, "Terze rime", and in 1580, she published her libertine letters, "Lettere familiari a diversi", which were in danger of being placed on the Index of books banned by the Church. Veronica eventually went down in history, for a spectacular entrance she staged for King Henry III; she had herself served to him on an oversized plate, wearing nothing but her birthday suit and her natural beauty, as a sumptuous snack. The performance must have been impressive, because for centuries Veronica's name remained a by-word for a top-class Venetian courtesan.

Address Parrocchia of the Chiesa di Sant'Agnese, Campo di Sant Agnese, Dorsodurdo, 30123 Venice | **Vaporetto fermata** Zattere, line B, 2, 5.1/5.2, 6, 8, 10, 16, night route N | **Tip** Not far from the Parrocchia you'll also find the slightly less well-known Calle Franchi, another reminder of Veronica Franco's honourable family.

58__The Footprints
Bridge of fists

Stepping onto the Pugni bridge, opposite the eponymous Osteria Pugni, you can make out two white footprints of Istrian stone on each side of the plateau. Known as "sampe" in the Venetian dialect, they are a reminder that this bridge was once used as a kind of boxing ring, where enemy neighbourhoods would enact various fights. These battles were usually organised between September and Christmas and followed a fixed ritual with a "Godfather" as referee. First the individual fights would take place, followed by collective fights, as they were known, with two to five participants on each side, and eventually anybody who felt like it was allowed to join in.

While the individual and collective fights more or less resembled traditional ring or fist fights, with fixed rules, group fights followed a slightly different choreography. Participants attempted to conquer space on the bridge by attacking and surging forward. No rules applied here – everything and anything was allowed, even kicking or low blows.

As the bridges at the time were "without cheeks", i.e. had no railings, many participants landed in the Canal. Victory went to the one who was first able to attach his flag to the highest point of the bridge.

Sometimes however, rivals were not just pushed into the water. In San Barnaba, a legendary fight took place in 1705 where both groups were throwing stones at each other, causing the altercation to take a bloody turn. The mass brawl subsequently morphed into a knife fight, with nobody noticing that a fire had broken out. The priest of San Barnaba managed in extremis to end the fight by waving a crucifix. Following this event, the Consilium Sapientis (Council of the Wise) decided to ban this venerable custom.

Address Ponte dei Pugni, Dorsoduro, 30123 Venice | Vaporetto fermata Ca' Rezzonico, line A, 1 | Tip In Venice there were several bridges used to act out fights such as these – including in Cannaregio on the bridge of Santa Fosca. Initially, the fights were supported by the Serenissima; the idea was that they kept the men in fighting shape, and provided an outlet for violent personalities. At the same time, the city would stoke the rivalry between the neighbourhoods, thus preventing them from fraternising – all in the sense of the Roman maxim "divide et impera" (divide and rule) – thus making them easier to control.

59__ The Nail

The invisible relic

Nearly all visitors of San Panthalon visit the church to view arguably the largest painting in the world, which – assembled from 40 individual panels – adorns the ceiling. But the Cappella del Santo Chiodo, too, is home to valuable art treasures, first and foremost, the shrine of the nail from the Crucifixion of Christ. Louis IX of France, no less, is said to have presented this valuable relic to the city in 1270. In any case, he handed over a ring and a small box to the Mother Superior of the Poor Clares of Santa Chiara at the time, and said the box's contents could only be given to somebody wearing an identical ring.

As Louis died in Tunis from an epidemic and didn't return, the nuns opened the little box, finding the nail together with an "expert report". According to this document, the nail came to be in the possession of Saint Helena over the course of the hunt for the Holy Cross. Helena's son, Constantine, brought the relic first to Rome, subsequently to Byzance and later to Constantinople. After the Crusaders' conquest of Constantinople in 1203, the French and Venetian victors divided up the relics of the Passion of Christ amongst themselves.

When the Poor Clares' convent was closed by Napoleon in 1810, the Mother Superior of the day, Sister Maria Lucarelli, fled into the Chiesa San Pantalon, gifting the relic to the church on 30 May 1830. On Good Friday, 1836, the Holy Nail was brought into the Cappella; since then it has been presented to the faithful on a yearly basis – unfortunately this tradition has not been able to continue as in 2012 the nail was stolen.

Still, you can imagine the holy relic – its shrine and a replica are on view at least. And the other art treasures, including a relief showing the Entombment of Christ, the Paradiso painting by Giovanni di Almagna and the fresco of the Black Madonna are all well worth seeing.

Address Cappella del Santo Chiodo (in the Chiesa di San Pantalon), Campo San Pantalon, Dorsoduro 3765, 30123 Venice | **Opening times** Daily 4–6pm (check with staff beforehand to visit the chapel) | **Vaporetto fermata** San Tomà, line 1, 2, night route N | **Tip** The level of madness that Venice displayed in its thirst for relics is also demonstrated in the huge collection of relics, some very eccentric, that are kept in Saint Mark's. Amongst the curiosities is a vial with the blood of Christ, a small part of the pillar where Christ was scourged, the arm of Saint George that he used to kill the dragon (see page 28), and a relic with the Milk of the Holy Virgin.

60__The Rio Terà dei Gesuati
A filled-in canal

Roughly translated, the Venetian phrase "Rio Terà" means something like "Earth River". Leaving aside Jesus Christ here, as hardly anyone has been or is able to walk on water, these "walkable canals" had to be filled in with soil. The Rio Terà dei Gesuati, near the Jesuates church, is a good example of such a former canal, with its remains still easily made out.

Canals have played a fundamental role in Venice since the city's foundation. Around the year 1500, the network of canals comprised over 37 kilometres/23 miles, fulfilling several functions: serving as a transport and communications artery, to supply food as well as waste disposal and last but not least, it had to be ensured that fresh water could circulate in the lagoon.

Before the end of the 18th century hardly any canals had been filled in. To the contrary, actually – people were forever creating new waterways. Filling in a canal was only considered in an emergency situation, when there was simply no other alternative. Though even in cases like this, the preferred option was to span the canal with a vault whenever possible, rather than abandoning it. Nevertheless, in 1156 the Rio Batario had to be filled in, to establish what is today's St Mark's Square.

After the fall of the Serenissima, in 1797, a different perspective prevailed; the main aim was to modernise the city. Over six kilometres/nearly four miles of canal were filled in (representing 20 per cent of the overall length of the canals at the time), and by around 1866, 30 per cent of the canals were no longer in existence. Luckily, the operation ended just in time, allowing Venice to remain a city of water. Faced with the lack of sufficient mooring sites for boats today, digging up some of these canals once again is being discussed. One positive side effect would be improved water circulation in the lagoon.

Address Fondamenta delle Zattere ai Gesuati, Dorsoduro 917, 30123 Venice (on the wall of the church of Santa Maria del Rosario, of the Jesuates monastery) | **Vaporetto fermata** Zattere, line B, 2, 5.1/5.2, 6, 8, 10, 16, night route N | **Tip** The Rio del Santissimo is the only subterranean canal in Venice, leading beneath the choir of the church of Santo Stefano and navigable by boat or gondola.

61_ The Squero
The invention of single-handed steering

In many travel guides you can read that the picturesque Squero (gondola yard) opposite the church of San Trovaso is the last remaining shipyard here. In truth, there are more, even if some only take care of repair work and others even function on a voluntary basis, in order to preserve historic boats.

Arguably the most important squero is the Domenico Tramontin & Figli company, on Ponte Sartorio, as it was this firm that started developing and building the first asymmetrical gondolas in the 1880s. The gondolas' starboard side was shortened by a quarter of a metre compared to the port side, and the resulting bend of the hulk allowed the gondola to be rowed by a single gondolier, moving the oar on the right-hand side. Up to that point gondolas had always been rowed by two or four men, standing at the stern or the prow.

While we're on the subject of the prow: the prow iron is an allegory of Venice and represents, first of all, the districts (six rectangular fingers at the front for San Marco, San Polo, Santa Croce, Castello, Dorsoduro, Cannaregio and one pointing backwards for the Giudecca); second, the Doges (Capello del Doge is the name given to the large head); third, the Canal Grande (the iron forming an "S", representing the Canal, from the top to the lowest point at the hulk); and finally, the lower arch at the Capello is associated with the Rialto Bridge.

Also, the gondolas weren't always black – on the contrary: the wealthier their owner, the more magnificent their features. In the mid-18th century however the gondolas, too, fell victim to the anti-luxury laws (see page 12) and their appearance became regulated by law. They had to be a consistent black colour, allowing only the silver "ferro" (prow iron) and the golden sea horses and mermaids on either side to remain. Since then, the gondolas have existed in mournful uniformity.

Address Domenico Tramontin & Figli, Dorsoduro 1542, 30123 Venice, www.tramontingondole.it | **Vaporetto fermata** San Basilio, line 2, 5.1/5.2, 8, night route N | **Tip** The Squero di San Trovaso mentioned at the beginning is, in fact, both a repair yard as well as a kind of museum. No description is complete without mentioning the eminently complex "frocole" (rowlocks) for the oars, usually carved from walnut, pear or cherry wood. Every one of the notches and protrusions of a forcola serves a very specific purpose during manoeuvring. One of the last "remèri" (oar makers) is Carli Succ. Di P. Brandolisio, whose shop is located in Calle Rotta 4725. For a special shopping experience, head for Piero Dri's "Il Forcolaio Matto" in Cannaregio 4231 (www.ilforcolaiomatto.it).

62__ The Former Convento

An example of a meaningful conversion

No, the photograph is not staged – and, yes, this is the garden surrounding the back of the former convent next to the Chiesa S.S. Cosma e Damiano. A dream-like quiet reigns here; a sheltered leafy ambience. And, if you're lucky, you might meet one of the resident artists at work. Who knows, they may even wave you over and offer you an ombra.

The former convent is a good example of the city's policy of not only converting unoccupied buildings into luxury hotels, but also occasionally (if probably too rarely) creating meaningful new purposes for old edifices.

The convent of Cosma e Damiano fell victim to Napoleon's secularisation purges and was subsequently never restored. For a long time the building stood empty, until the city of Venice redeveloped a dozen flats here and, as part of the cultural revitalisation of the Giudecca neighbourhood, gave studios to five young artists who are using the spaces around the beautiful courtyard for creative purposes.

The adjacent church now houses a modern art gallery, with the space completely redesigned to accomodate exhibitions.

The former chapter house of the convent, known as the Sala del Camino, owes its name to its fine Renaissance-style chimney. It was rededicated and today serves as a space for art galleries and artists from Giudecca to meet and showcase their work, but is also used for various other events.

Most artists need peace and quiet to work, which is why tourists are not really welcome here; still, it's possible to catch a discreet glimpse of the lovely courtyard through the entrance gate. Those who'd like to visit will have to make friends with one of the artists, as they make much use of the garden.

Address Former convent S.S. Cosma e Damiano, Giudecca 620, 30133 Venice | Opening times The convent is not open to the public (but here is a little tip on how to get in for visitors interested in finely crafted goblets from Murano glass – send an email to muranoglassfineart@yahoo.com) | Vaporetto fermata Giudecca Palanca, line 2, 4.1/4.2, 8, night route N | Tip Santa Eufemia is also worthy of a visit; the pillars of its portico are said to come from the S.S. Biago e Cataldo monastery, which was torn down to make way for the Stucky Mill (see page 138). A commemorative plaque tells this particular tale.

63__ The Garden of Eden
What remains of paradise?

The area behind Giudecca's men's prison harbours one of Venice's best-kept secrets, which, through numerous stories, myths and semi truths, has become the incarnation of a garden legend. We are talking about the legendary "Garden of Eden", the former refuge of iconic Austrian artist, Friedrich Hundertwasser, who bought the estate in 1972, after it had been badly damaged in the great floods of 1966.

Yet it wasn't the paradisaical Garden of Eden that lent the space its name, but its first owner, a British gentleman by the name of Sir Frederick Eden, who had an English landscaped garden laid out here in 1885. At the time, this garden was so famous that for a long while it was considered a true wonder of the landscape gardening world.

Being able to visit the garden would be close to a miracle – still, you may be able to get a fleeting glimpse over the wall and see that, while the garden is no longer well-kept, it has not totally gone to seed either. On rare occasions – far and few between – gardeners will come in and take care of the most urgent maintenance requirements, primarily fighting the rampant weeds. This, however, would not have been to the liking of Hundertwasser. The artist was of the opinion that a garden could only be paradisiacal if no gardening took place, leaving nature to do its thing. His name for this was "spontaneous vegetation".

Still, Hundertwasser would occasionally pitch in, pulling out nettles, announcing with conviction: "You know how easy it is to live without money? Simply eat nettles. Nettles grow everywhere, and they are completely free – dig in!"

If nettles form the main diet in paradise, it's probably not a place you'd want to enter; and if you did end up there, the temptation of an apple would quickly prove irresistible!

Address Fondamenta al Rio della Croce, Giudecca, 30133 Venice (the garden is located at the eastern end; the gate with the Garden of Eden inscription is situated before the bridge, on the right-hand side) | **Vaporetto fermata** Redentore, line 2, 4.1/4.2, 8, night route N | **Tip** Those wanting to ignore Hundertwasser's recommendation, and go for fish or seafood instead, should head for the Ristorante al Storico da Crea, where typically Venetian cuisine can be enjoyed with a view of the large shipyard, as well as the lagoon (www.ristorantealstorico.com).

64__The Ponte dei Lavraneri

Traces of industrial Venice

Coming from Sacca Fisola and crossing the Ponte dei Lavraneri heading towards the Giudecca, you can make out an old chimney between the very modern lanterns of the bridge (made from laminated wood), which once was a part of the local Fabbrica Birra Venezia factory. Even though the traditional brewery is now back in operation in Mestre decades after shutting down, only fragments remain of the former wealth of this industry in Venice.

Indeed, it's hard to believe, that the Giudecca was ever once a centre of agriculture and industry. Today, most of the former industrial facilities house flats, hotels, and even theatres. The former brewery, too, was converted into flats, right adjacent to the former Stucky Mill that today serves as a monumentally elegant brick framework for a famous luxury hotel (see page 138).

What has been preserved, at least, is the workshop of Spanish fashion designer, Fortuny, who in the early 20th century moved from the Campo Sant'Angelo to the Giudecca, where he has been creating his fabulous fabrics ever since.

Many of the industrial workshops emerging in Venice in the 19th and 20th centuries in particular, were established on the Giudecca, especially those run by foreigners. One of the foreign entrepreneurs was a German named Herion, who ran a yarn and textile production outfit here in the former monastery of Cosma e Damiano. Today, the monastery serves young artists as a studio space (see page 132). The most lasting trace – at least concerning the name – was left by the equally German Junghans factory, which produced precision instruments such as clocks, timers and, in times of war, hand bomb detonators too. The land of the Junghans factory was later used in the development of flats, a residence hall for students, and a theatre, all located on what today is called Campo Junghans.

Address Ponte dei Lavraneri, Giudecca, 30133 Venice | **Vaporetto fermata** Molino Stucky, line B; Giudecca Hilton, line B | **Tip** At the Vaporetto stop of "Giudecca Palanca", number 595 has a cast-iron gate – behind which the last ropeyard of Venice was operating up until the 1990s. The lane behind cuts in an almost straight line nearly the entire width of the Giudecca. More traces of industrial Venice can be found at the railway station and the Piazzale Roma (see page 72).

65__ The Stucky Bust
How to blackmail a city

Some Venetians like to complain about the sellout going on in their city, about the large-scale investors destroying everything (it's not quite clear what, really, as there is hardly a conservation authority as strict as the Italian one) and converting Venice into a Disneyworld for the super rich. However, wasn't it always thus? Haven't the noble and wealthy folk from all over the world always invested in Venice and left their mark on the city as they saw fit?

Venice has always been a city of commerce and money, and what the Venetians didn't sell they gambled away at the card table – and nobody's ever complained. And which investor or company could buy a palazzo if there weren't any available for sale? Still, there are limits to everything, good taste in particular, and sometimes the line gets crossed. A good example of such a transgression is the former Stucky Mill. The huge building was erected by a Swiss man, Stucky, who was already running a smaller mill in Venice and looking to expand operations. Initially, the Venetians weren't thrilled about his plans for this monster box of a building, yet Stucky was able to convince them to let him build his mega mill – he simply threatened to fire all employees and staff if the venture wasn't authorised. This argument had such power that the city issued the building permit.

The mill was in operation until 1955 when the whole story started ed again: first a Sicilian, subsequently arrested for fraud, acquired the industrial monument, announcing the construction of flats. Then, in a surprising turn of events, the mill – affected by some "insignificant" touch of arson – was converted into a luxury hotel.

What the Venetians seem to object to, is not the investment and commercial activity of the wealthy in itself, but more the arrogance and superiority that Stucky and his ilk display – and it is exactly this arrogance that is expressed in Stucky's bust.

Address Molino Stucky Hilton, Giudecca 810, 30133 Venice (the bust stands behind the hotel in the courtyard in front of the spa area) | Vaporetto fermata Molino Stucky, line B; Giudecca Hilton, line B | Tip Even though some too conservatively-minded nostalgic merchants won't like it – the Sky Bar on the top floor of the Stucky Mulino Hilton is a true hot spot. And the Hilton group has managed, despite all the quarrelling in the back story, to create a location that can claim to represent a modern Venice, without smothering the old (www.molinostuckyhilton.it).

66_ The Villa Herriot

Some rest for the soul

The Giudecca forms its own enchanted world, far from the maddening crowd of tourists between Rialto and San Marco. If you didn't know that you were on an island popularly known as "spina longa" you might think you were in some sleepy northern Italian village.

One of these particularly quiet spots is the garden of the Villa Herriot. While this is the location of a primary school and an international art university, asking nicely and behaving unobtrusively earns visitors the right to enjoy the incredible magic of this place too.

Dating back to 1929, Villa Herriot is a neo-Byzantine – some like to call it neo-Gothic – edifice, hidden in the maze of alleys behind the Citadel. The villa consists of two buildings, one of which is open to discreet visitors. What is surprising is the design of the hall, more reminiscent of a small hunting lodge than the residence of a Venetian patrician family. Various weapons hang on the walls, with the visual focal point provided by a fine statue representing the Archangel, Michael.

The villa was originally built for a Frenchman, Herriot, as a holiday residence. In 1947 his widow gave the city the estate under the condition that it would be converted into a school – which is why the Carlo Goldoni primary school was established here. The "Università Internationale dell'Arte" (UIA, a university specialising in restorations) as well as the "Società Europea di Cultura" (European Cultural Society), too, honour the last will and testament of Lady Herriot.

The most important reason for coming here is, without a doubt, the beautiful garden, yielding magnificent views of the southern lagoon; the impression you get is that the sea is literally at your feet.

Address Villa Herriot, Calle Michelangelo 54/P, Giudecca, 30133 Venice | Opening times Mon–Fri (Tue and Thu) 10am–1pm | Vaporetto fermata Zitelle, line B, 2, 4.1/4.2, 8, night route N | Tip Don't miss the vegetable garden of the Capuchin monastery; its entrance is to the left at the back, next to the Redentore church – the garden may be visited after a polite phone request (0039/415224348).

67__ The Chiesa di San Gerardo

And if Venice was a normal city after all?

The island of Sacca Fisola is of more recent vintage; as you can see on older maps of the city, in the 19th century it wasn't even there – only salt marshes existed. Sacca Fisola was created from landfill ("sacca" is the name given to an island originating from artificial soil deposits). This is a Venice far from any tourist crowds; you'll find groceries, textile stores, football fields (see photograph), down-to-earth bars that don't force you to constantly keep an eye on your budget, shops selling everyday items, and everything else that makes up a regular small town in Italy. Even trucks may on occasion enter Sacca Fisola, but only to supply the weekly market – in Venice, this is something rather special.

Another place of particular interest is the Chiesa di San Gerardo, not in an artistic or architectural sense, more in a historical sense – the edifice, a result of the building boom of the 1970s, is an example of the fact that even Venice has never been totally protected from eyesores, nor will it be in the future.

It might be unsettling to think that not even this city is immune to less than attractive buildings, yet Venice too must be allowed to modernise and to evolve with the times – just like any other city; otherwise even more locals will move out. The ones doing the complaining are usually the foreign visitors, even though they are not the ones living here and are able to enjoy all the modern conveniences available in their hotels.

Venice has changed and will continue to do so – and that's great! To decide the way in which it changes has to be left to the Venetians; after all, it is still their home.

On the other hand, overwhelming beauty should be preserved, of course. How did Austrian writer Torberg's famous character, Aunt Jolesch, phrase it? "All cities are equal, only Venice is a bit different!"

Address Chiesa di San Gerardo, Campo san Gerardo/Campiello Chiesa, Giudecca/Sacca Fisola, 30133 Venice | **Vaporetto fermata** Sacca Fisola, line 2, 4.1/4.2, 8, night route N | **Tip** Another nice indication that Venice can also be a completely "normal" city is the fact that there is a public indoor pool (Piscina Comunale), on the island of Sacca Fisola. There is a slight drawback however: it has one pool, for swimmers only, making it unsuitable for non-swimmers or toddlers (tel. 0039/415285430).

68__ The Lion and the Venus
A fresco's city history

There is a building facade in Campiello del Teatro in Saca, which features a remarkable fresco dominated by a winged lion and a young girl. What is odd is the empty, near ghostly face of the lion, which seems mask-like, soulless and not of this world. And the lion doesn't appear to just want to block the sun, but also to dominate an agonising Venus begging for help – and in fact, this is something that happened for real in the city's history. The symbol of today's Venice is no longer Venus, but the lion, an allusion to Mark the Evangelist.

Legend tells us that today's Venice was founded on 25 March 811, under the sign of Venus (see page 182). Venus was the daughter of the moon and the sister of the sun; her mother ruled the underworld, and the waters of the lagoon along with the crocodile reportedly living in it. This is why Venice put so much effort into finding the bones of Saint Mark, as the name Mark has Indo-Germanic roots, and "Makara" means – crocodile!

Since 828, the relics of the Evangelist have been in repose in Venice. The Serenissima took on the name Serenissima Repubblica di San Marco and has featured the Lion of St Mark in its coat of arms ever since.

So this is the explanation for the fresco: St Mark, patron saint of Venice, is celebrated on 25 April, when the sun (usually symbolised by a lion – which is why the lion in the fresco is standing in the sun) enters the constellation of Taurus (witness the bull next to Venus), which is ruled by Venus.

Venus also represents the astrological sign of Virgo and the other signs of the zodiac complementing it may be identified too. Looking at the social context on the Giudecca you'll now understand that this astrological sign fresco is critical of the city of Venice – as this lion is not only faceless, it's also blind!

Address Campiello del Teatro in Saca, 30133 Venice (it's impossible to miss the fresco on the wall of the house) | **Vaporetto fermata** Sacca Fisola, line 2, 4.1/4.2, 8, night route N | **Tip** The Palazzo Agnusdio on Fondamenta Pesaro 2060 in Santa Croce features reliefs of all four Evangelists with their attributes: Mark (lion), John (eagle), Luke (ox) and Matthew (man/angel).

69 The Bistrot de Venise

Castradina and historical recipes

Well-versed connoisseurs of Venetian gastronomy are likely to have heard of the fine, Bistrot de Venise.

A few years ago they decided to restore a style of cooking that had hitherto disappeared from Venice: the historical dishes of the Doges and Patricians.

New interpretations of recipes from the cookbook of an unknown Venetian chef, as well as Bartolomeo Scappi's culinary artistry, form the Bistrot de Venise's menu and are complemented with recipes by other legendary Venetian cooks of the 14th to 18th centuries.

In this way, the restaurant takes its guests on a unique culinary trip back in time, travelling through the pots of Venice, reviving the historical scents and aromas of the Serenissima.

A rather special feast may be enjoyed on 21 November, the day of Madonna della Salute, as this is celebrated with the traditional "castradina", a rustic stew with salted, slightly smoked and air-dried mutton ham, a specialty from the southern Dalmatian coast, where this dish was created. Visually, castradina resembles an Irish stew and is cooked for hours on a low flame, developing a lovely aroma of thyme.

Another classic now revived in contemporary cooking is the "anatra arrosto con la salsa peverada", a wild duck braised in the oven with a deliciously aromatic liver sauce.

As fine food in Venice often means "reassuringly expensive", the concept of this establishment is definitely also aimed at a clientele that likes to discreetly ignore the right-hand side of the menu. Still, this, too, fits with the mentality of wealthy Venice, as they didn't just enjoy making money, but always also spending it, in the most stylish and grand way possible, a notion that Casanova subscribed to as well.

Address Calle dei Fabbri, San Marco 4685, 30124 Venice, tel. 0039/415236651, www.bistrotdevenise.com | **Opening times** Daily 12 noon–3pm and 7pm–midnight | Vaporetto fermata Rialto, line A, 1, 2, night route N | **Tip** The castradina is closely connected with the history of the church of "Madonna della Salute" in Dorsoduro. In the mid-17th century, the plague was raging in the once so lively city, decimating it terribly. In 1631, a promise was made to erect a church if the heavens were to come to the city's rescue. After the end of the plague, a settlement of shacks was torn down to build the votive church of "Madonna della Salute", which was inaugurated on 21 November after 20 years of construction. To this day, this feast day is celebrated every year.

70_ The Cucina da Mario

Canteen of the gondolieri

If you visit the rustic and cosy Cucina da Mario at lunchtime you'll have the opportunity (usually anyway) to have your "pranzo" (lunch) together with gondolieri, as they frequent da Mario's as something like a canteen.

It's a nice experience, the gondolieri ensuring a unique ambience – and without the usual "prezzi salati" (hefty prices) one has to fork out for a gondola trip. Oversized wine bottles occupy nearly all the tables, probably contributing to the good spirits of these guests, clad in red-and-white or blue-and-white shirts.

Don't think for a minute that the gondolieri choose these shirts by sheer coincidence – the clothing of this profession, like many things in Venice, is regulated.

Article 23 of the "Regolamneto Comunale per il Servizio Pubblico di Gondola", the municipal decree for occupations in public service of the gondolas, stipulates the requirement for these uniforms. The gondolieri have to dress following the protocol of their profession.

In the winter season this means long navy or black trousers without side pockets, paired with dark-blue or black sailor tops. Wearing a soft cap with or without a tassle or a bobble hat of the same colour is permitted.

In the case of severe cold weather, the men are also allowed to wear a black or dark-blue coat; and when it rains they can don a "cerata in tinta" (wet-weather jacket).

In the summer season, the gondoliere also has to wear long trousers in dark-blue or black, a white linen shirt, sailor-style, or a "maglietta" (t-shirt) with horizontal red or blue stripes 2 to 2.5 centimetres wide, and a straw hat with a ribbon and lining in the same colour as the shirt. Regulation footwear is closed-toe black shoes.

Address Fondamenta della Prefettura, San Marco 2614, 30124 Venice, tel. 0039/415285968 | **Opening times** 10.30am–3pm and 6.30–10pm | **Vaporetto fermata** Giglio, line A, 1 | **Tip** Apart from the name, the Ristorante ai Gondolieri in Dorsoduro 366 has nothing much in common with the gondolieri. Specialising in Venetian meat dishes, it is, however, one of the best in Venice.

71__ The Devil's Hole

How to chase a devil

There is a story behind that strange angel standing at the back of the Palazzo Soranzo and pointing to a large hole in the upper third of the house wall: in 1552, a lawyer living in this palace was making a fortune with dodgy dealings, even though he liked to call himself a pious and honest man.

One evening, he invited the monk, Matteo de Bascio, for dinner, showing off his tame monkey who was able to perform all kinds of household duties. When the monk saw the animal he immediately recognised the demon in it and asked him what he thought he was doing there. The Devil explained that he was waiting for the soul of the lawyer, to take it back to hell with him. However, he hadn't been successful, thus far, because the lawyer was praying to the Virgin Mary every evening. As soon as the lawyer forgot to pray, his soul would be forsaken.

On hearing this, de Bascio ordered the Devil to leave the house immediately. However, the Devil retorted that he could only do so if the monk allowed him to wreak havoc on the house. De Bascio agreed, under the condition that he would be the one to decide the extent of the damage. The deal was agreed upon and the Devil disappeared through the wall, leaving the hole in the wall.

The monk then spoke to the lawyer in earnest, reproaching him for his many sins and transgressions. Eventually the monk took a corner of the tablecloth, wrung it out, and the blood from those exploited by the lawyer began dripping onto the floor. The lawyer showed repentance and vowed to improve upon his ways. He also expressed his worry that the Devil could use the hole to come back into the house. Matteo calmed him down and recommended that he simply erect a statue of an angel near the hole, which would chase away any evil spirit.

Address Facade of Palazzo Soranzo, San Marco, 30124 Venice (best to turn into the Calle de la Canonica first, then take the first street on the left; after 50 metres you'll be at the Ponte dell'Angelo; the best place to see the facade.) | **Vaporetto fermata** San Marco, line A, B, R, 2, 10, night route N | **Tip** A good dining option if you're coming from the Piazza San Marco along the way to the Devil's Hole, is the Pizzeria Rossopomodoro (www.venezia.rossopomodoro.it), serving original Neapolitan pizza baked in a wood-fired oven decorated with small golden mosaic tiles. Enjoy the fun rustic wooden armchairs with recipes for Neapolitan cuisine written on their backrests.

72__ The Fiorella Gallery
The art of provocation

"Clothes are like masks: protecting us from reality!", says Fiorella Mancini, who runs an eccentric and provocative blend of gallery, boutique and fashion salon on Campo Santo Stefano.

The not entirely uncontroversial designer is one of the most dazzling personalities on the contemporary art scene. Fiorella Mancini not only designs quirky fashion, she also makes political statements with her collections – especially on subjects that are usually quite taboo in Venice.

Fiorella campaigns for the full acceptance of homosexuality in society, for instance; in 2005 she held an "anti Biennale" in her gallery, where under the light of a shrill neon tube with the inscription "Bed & Breakfeast", two men in underpants spent five days lounging on a bed in the window, offering up an alternative reality show.

One of the favourite motifs of this adventurous designer is rats. To be fair, it's not only the artist who has a special relationship with these rodents, it's the city of Venice. Rats can be found on Fiorella's jackets, underpants and coats.

One day Mancini took a boat through the canals of Venice, in the style of a Rhenish carnival float, with an over-sized rat aboard. She was doing this in protest against the environmental pollution in the city, and the sleaze of corruption. Everywhere, she says, the rats have taken control.

That's definitely the case in Venice's canals; the most recent estimates reckon there are five rats to every Venetian. Extremely adaptable, the rodents, small or large, have become perfectly accustomed to life in the city's obscure system of canals – and the cats, ever fewer due to sterilisation, are no longer a match for the huge army of rats, an image that can actually be taken literally.

Address Campo Santo Stefano, San Marco 2806, 30124 Venice, Tel. 0039/415209228, www.fiorellagallery.com | **Opening times** Mon–Sat 10.30am–7pm | **Vaporetto fermata** Accademia, line 1, 2, night route N | **Tip** The cylindrical stone plinth standing at the end of Calle del Traghetto in Cannaregio, exactly opposite the Canal Grande, bears the engraving of a rat with the year 1644. This "artwork" is of a much more recent date, however, aiming to point out that rats have been a part of the history of the city for centuries – according to legend, rats arrived by ship from faraway plague-ridden countries and were thus blamed for the plague epidemics of past centuries.

73__ The Golden Head

Guarding the celestial medicine

At the foot of the Rialto bridge, where tourist shops and souvenir stalls jostle for space, on the side of the San Bartolomeo church you can make out a golden head seemingly free-floating in the air. In truth, this head of gold is actually a bronze figure and used to be the emblem of the former pharmacy, Alla Testa d'Oro.

In times when few could read, the head adorned with a crown of laurels (probably representing Nero's personal physician, Andromachos) would indicate that golden knowledge could be found here. The strict facial features with the serious gaze of a personal guard convey the strong desire to keep and guard the mythical secret recipe for a miracle cure.

The wall still bears the faded fragment of an inscription revealing what was produced here, in the strictest secrecy: "theriaca andromachi" – the famous celestial drug, the legendary theriak (see page 166), able to heal any illness.

This pharmacy specialised in the preparation of this medicine in 1603, and according to reports, the best theriak in town was made here. It was for this reason that the Golden Head pharmacy was also given permission to make the unique drug, prepared according to an incredibly complex ritual, three times per year – while all others were only allowed to engage in its preparation once a year.

Following the fall of the Republic of Venice in 1797, the pharmacy was the only one continuing to produce the unusual curative up until the end of the past century. However, from 1940 onwards, the opiate from the original recipe had to be left out of the concoction, much to the chagrin of the patients, as opiates, we know, alleviate pain.

Today, this place, formerly the last refuge of theriak, has been consigned to history too.

Address Salizada Pio X, Rialto, San Marco, 30124 Venice | Vaporetto fermata Rialto, line 2, night route N | Tip To see a well-preserved historic pharmacy that's still operating, head for the Antica Farmacia Santa Fosca in Strada Nuova no. 2233, next to the Spezeria all'Ercole d'Oro.

74__ The High Altar

Dance around the golden calf

One of the oldest churches in Venice, the Chiesa San Moise, was first mentioned in the 8th century. In 947 it was redesigned by the Patrician, Moisè Valier, who renamed the church for his patron saint, Moses. The church kept being plagued by fire; the last time this happened, in 1632, the whole edifice had to be reconstructed. What has remained, though, is its name and the Old Testament story connected with Moses, which explains the altar relief, fairly unusual for a church.

Visitors to the church will certainly be a little surprised to find such provocative representations of the famous tale of the Golden Calf, on an altar of all places. On the right-hand side, a happy crowd is dancing around the idol (the golden calf), and in the centre you see two women making music, with one of them clearly holding a rhythm instrument in her hand. This is significant because in Antiquity, rhythm instruments were nearly exclusively played by women during what was known as symposiums (think drinking orgies). The reference to the debauched symposium is there, on the left-hand side of the altar, where the relief shows a "hetaera", or educated courtesan, in an orgiastic trance, with a number of folk behind her drinking and eating heartily.

Now it might not come as too much of a surprise to find this story that's connected to Moses in a church dedicated to him – however, the fact that there is not a single reference to Moses, himself, Mount Sinai, the Tablets of Law or the Ten Commandments, only a glorification of the debauched orgy around the Golden Calf, is more than simply notable. Somehow, though, this altar fits in well with Venice's anti-church and anti-Pope stance and its relaxed attitude towards religion. Indeed, it seems that religion was far less restrictively practised than the official church would have liked.

Address Chiesa San Moisè, Salita San Moisè, San Marco, 30124 Venice (relief on the high altar) | **Opening times** Mon–Sat 9.30am–12.30pm and 1–4.30pm, Sun 9.30–11am and 1–6.30pm | **Vaporetto fermata** San Marco, line A, 1, 2, 10, night route N | **Tip** Visitors to the church of San Moise who keep their eyes peeled can look forward to more surprises – the choir stalls around the altar are adorned with bare-bosomed ladies. There is a definite erotic charge emanating from the famous Tintoretto painting, which depicts Jesus washing the disciples' feet, carefree bare-bosomed ladies showing off their wares to best advantage, and men caught in sexual ecstasy vying for a place near the seductive rounded white flesh. How does the verse in the Bible put it – the people sat down to eat, drink and got up to amuse themselves?

75_ The Holy Nipple

A semi-disrobed Mary Magdalene

The church of Santa Maria del Giglio is a curiosity in its own right, as only looking at the imaginatively designed facade makes you feel that you're in front of a building belonging to a university or chamber of commerce, rather than a holy site. The city maps outlining Venice's most important trading partners, in particular, are something you wouldn't expect to see in a place such as this. The church of Santa Maria del Giglio is the seat of the Order of the Knights of the Holy Sepulchre, whose main job is to represent the interests of the Catholic church in Jerusalem and to guard the crown of thorns crown kept in Notre Dame in Paris – you'll see the cross of the Order adorning the entrance door.

Stepping into this strange church, don't miss the paintings of the Evangelists behind the altar; they are well worth seeing and include two paintings by Tintoretto, representing Saint Mark and Saint Matthew.

The sanctuary for the relics, to the right of the entrance, displays fine artefacts, with a fragment of the veil of the Virgin Mary probably being the most interesting. Particularly remarkable is also the ivory sculpture of Mary Magdalene at the foot of the Cross, not only for her sensual near-erotic gaze (despite her mourning), but also for her uncovered left nipple.

During the baroque era in particular, Maria Magdalene was often represented as a counterpoint to the chaste Mary, usually as the beautiful repentant sinner. Not the least of her functions was – just like Eve – to serve as an excuse for artists to show an erotic naked woman, sexy and sexually arousing, and in Christian art too. So Mary Magdalene was often represented as Woman; with wild hair, sparkling eyes, a seductive body – lustful, sensual and naked as God made her.

Address Santa Maria del Giglio, Campo Santa Maria del Giglio, San Marco, 30124 Venice (sanctuary of relics) | **Opening times** Mon–Sat 10am–5pm | **Vaporetto fermata** Santa Maria del Giglio, line A, 1 | **Tip** The same sanctuary allows visitors to admire the beautiful Rubens painting "Virgin with Child" and "John the Baptist as a Boy", the only painting by the artist in the city – again, the voluptuous, shapely uncovered left breast of the Virgin seems so sensual and erotic that it's hard to believe that the artist was only thinking of breastfeeding.

76__The Lord Byron Plaque

The amorous adventures of the poet

In 1818 the poet Lord Byron, already famous at the time, rented the Palazzo Mocenigo, where he was to stay for two years, leading a life shrouded in scandal. In September of that year he moved in, together with 14 house staff, eight dogs, five cats, two monkeys, a fox and countless birds stuffed into cages. The following years were dominated by an exciting lifestyle, primarily characterised by wild romantic escapades, debauched orgies, illicit liaisons and countless affairs.

Byron's amorous adventures were the talk of the town, and his charm broke the heart of many a Venetian lady – few were able to withstand the advances of the smart Englishman. People joked that the Palazzo Mocenigo needed two entrances: one for the girls from Cannaregio, and another for those from Castello.

Thirty years old at the time, Lord Byron was not merely famous for the power of his loins, but also for his eccentric lifestyle. Apart from lavish parties, the sports-mad poet also organised competitions, such as a swimming event leading from the Lido into the city and through the entire Canal Grande.

With the authorisation of the Austrian governor, Byron was also allowed to keep horses on the Lido and he never tired of boasting that the only horses in Venice apart from those in front of St Mark's Basilica, were his own.

Documenting his reputation as an enfant terrible, Byron regaled all his passionate exploits in letters to friends. However, apart from all this, he did also do some work. He wrote a lot, in fact, allowing the Venetian local colour to inspire him.

The finest work from this creative period has to be his play "The Two Foscari", which later served as a libretto for Verdi's eponymous opera.

Address Palazzo Mocenigo (il Nero), Calle Mocenigo Casa Nova, 30124 Venice (the commemorative plaque is only visible from the Canal) | **Vaporetto fermata** Sant Angelo, line A, 1 | Tip Passing the Palazzo Mocenigo by Vaporetto, you can see across the way – slightly set back into a side canal – the terrace where the Brunetti family has their meals in the TV version of the famous Donna Leon thrillers.

77__ The Lovers

A stone book at the Doge's Palace

The Doge's Palace was not only the centre of government and a symbol of the greatness and power of Venice, it also worked as a kind of picture book, an attempt to instruct the population, most of whom could not read or write, about important happenings and relationships.

The palace has 600 capitals, depicting the story of Genesis, handing out slices of moral teaching through allegory, telling short stories and mythology, showing the holy as much as the secular, as well as mirroring the sublimity of God, of course.

The Biblical corner sculptures (The Fall of Adam and Eve, Noah's Drunkenness and Solomon's Judgment) are larger than the others, emphasising as they do the political direction of the Republic, resting on the Christian faith.

Some of the smaller capitals in the arcades are much more secular in nature, showing birds and their prey, for instance, important kings and emperors, beautiful Roman ladies, the peoples of the Earth, the Seven Arts (grammar, arithmetic, dialectics, rhetoric, geometry, music, astronomy) personified by the seven wise men, the planets, crafts, months and fruit.

Of course the picture wouldn't be complete without the deadly sins, which are represented by allegories: Gluttony as a shank of meat and wine, Wrath tearing its clothes off, Greed showing an old lady clutching a purse, Sloth in the clutches of apathy, Vanity surrounded by flowers ogled by an enraged Envy, and, yes, you guessed it, Lust represented by a young lady exposing her breast, while gazing at her mirror image in admiration.

And the circle of life too, is represented in stone: a man courting a woman, a man and a woman lying together, and the natural result – children, to serve as heirs.

Address Doge's Palace, Piazzetta San Marco, San Marco 1, 30124 Venice | Vaporetto fermata San Marco, line A, B, R, 2, 10 | Tip In the late 19th century, the 42 chapters (13 in the outer arch, 29 in the loggia) were replaced by copies – the originals may be admired today in the Museo dell'Opera of the Doge's Palace (open daily except on high public holidays 9am–6pm).

78__ The Man With No Arms
An odd engraving

Palazzo Loredan is one of the best-preserved Venetian-Byzantine palaces on the Canal and a typical "fondaco" (palace with warehouse and arches along the waterfront). The arches lend the facade a certain lightness, and every free spot is decorated with colourful marble.

Look at the second column from the left at the front of the palazzo and you'll be able to make out an engraving, representing a man with a long pipe. A closer look reveals that the man has no arms. To understand what's behind this engraving, you need to know the following legend: there was once a fisherman named Biagio, a good and well-liked gentleman who stopped on occasion in front of Palazzo Loredan to earn a little spare cash. During his few breaks, Biagio liked to sit alongside the Canal, to quietly smoke a pipe. One evening the fisherman noticed that the water below a passing gondola was turning a red colour. Two strong black arms with claws could be seen emerging from the water – no doubt, the Devil himself! The terrified gondoliere took flight, while the Devil tried to kidnap the two girls inside the "felze" (small cabin at the centre of a gondola). Throwing his pipe into the water, Biagio shouted at Satan with his arms spread wide apart – making the shape of a cross – to take him instead of the children. Satan taunted the fisherman for daring to imitate a cross with his arms, and responded that he'd only let the children go if his arms could span the whole world.

As soon as the devil had spoken those words, Biagio's arms disconnected from his body, as if by magic, without the fisherman feeling any pain. A flock of cherubim arrived, took hold of the arms and flew away with the sacrificial offering. As if hit by a massive blow, the devil desisted from his attack, and disappeared.

Address Palazzo Corner Piscopia Loredan, Riva del Carbon, San Marco, 30124 Venice | Vaporetto fermata Rialto, line A, 1, 2, night route N | Tip A commemorative plaque on the wall of Ca' Loredan honours the memory of Elena Lucrezia Cornaro Piscopia, who was born here in 1646 – the first woman to finish university on 25 June 1678; she is considered the first female academic.

79 The Mortar Imprint

A reminder of celestial medicine

On the corner between the Campo Santo Stefano and Calle del Spezier ("spezier da medicina" is the Venetian for "pharmacy") you can make out a perfectly circular imprint on the floor right opposite the pharmacy. This is where a large mortar used to stand, required for the preparation of theriak – the celestial medicine supposed to have helped against all kinds of diseases. Not any old pharmacist was allowed to manufacture theriak; only 40 of the 90 Venetian pharmacies of the time had the necessary authorisation. The remedy was prepared in the street in an oversize bronze mortar, and its imprint can still be seen at the place where it once stood.

To maintain the quality of the theriak, it was subject to strict regulations by the Republic – theriak could only be produced under the supervision of the health authorities, and all ingredients used had to be offered up to the gaze of the public, which was quite the spectacle, one of the main ingredients being live vipers.

In the first century BC, Mithridates, King of Pontos first developed a recipe for the miracle potion from 46 ingredients. Nero's personal physician Andromachos went on to complete this basic recipe with 25 additional ingredients. Kriton, Emperor Trajan's personal physician, in turn, gave the remedy its name, and the prominent Greek physician Galenus (131–201) was responsible for spreading its fame.

The most important ingredients were powder of vipers, opium, dried wine-stone, powder of deer testicles and ground narwhal horn. These creatures were also responsible for the remedy's name; theriak is derived from the Old Greek thēríon, meaning wild animal. Theriak helped against everything and anything: the plague, other infectious diseases, snakebites, tuberculosis, stomach complaints, fever, impaired vision and much more – just like a miracle cure should.

Address Campo Santo Stefano, in front of the building with the no. 2800, San Marco, 30124 Venice | Vaporetto fermata Accademia, line 1, 2, night route N | Tip In the past, the centre of the generously laid out Campo Santo Stefano served as a stage for numerous animal baiting events, with bullfights being particularly popular. The last one was staged in 1802, after which the spectacle was banned due to a collapsed staircase.

80_ The Old Woman with the Mortar

This high relief is a reminder of a conspiracy

The most famous shopping street in Venice, the Mercerie, has thousands of passers-by every day. Yet while the window displays of the luxury labels are extensively admired, most people overlook the interesting high relief on the corner of Sottoportego del Cappello. Showing an old woman with a mortar, it was commissioned in 1861 by a certain, Elia Vivante Mussati. It was affixed to the wall of the house as a reminder of the following event: on 15 June, 1310, the Tiepolo family, together with the Querinis and other noble families, were planning a conspiracy, instigated by Bajamonte Tiepolo (see page 204), with the aim of toppling Doge Pietro Gradenigo. The conspirators were betrayed, however, and were met by the waiting Doge's militia on St Mark's Square where a skirmish ensued. Eventually the conspirators had to accept defeat and start retreating. However, when the fleeing would-be usurpers came through the Mercerie they were recognised by an old lady called Lucia Rossi. A follower of the Doge, this lady threw her huge bronze mortar onto the conspirators from the height of her balcony, causing a lethal wound to the head of Querini, Tiepolo's standard-bearer.

Commercially-minded as the Venetians are, the lady did not hesitate to request a suitable reward. She asked for permission to fly the St Mark's flag every year on 15 June, as well as on major state occasions, and also for a freeze on the rent paid by her and her daughters. The Doge met these requests, even extending these privileges to all future descendants of the lady.

500 years later, Elia Vivante Mussati was still a happy beneficiary of these privileges and, out of gratitude, had the courtyard relief made showing the old woman throwing the mortar.

DDI XV GIVGNO MCC

Address Mercerie, at the corner with Sottoportego del Cappello, San Marco, 30124 Venice | **Vaporetto fermata** San Marco, line A, 1, 2, 10, night route N | **Tip** The flagpole of Campo San Luca bears symbols that also have a connection with the Tiepolo conspiracy: the coats of arms of two secular confraternities that helped make the conspiracy fail: the "Scuola della Carità" (of Charity) and the "Scuola dei Pittori" (of Painters).

81_ "Ombre"

Of light and dark shadows

"Ombra" is the Italian word for shadow and the Serenissima has more shady sides than the general public might think. Leaving aside environmental sins, Venice has always been a predatory city. The best example of this is the San Marco basilica, as its very name betrays the robbery that lies at its foundation – the theft of the bones of Saint Mark's, which were brought over from Egypt for political and tactical reasons. Or consider the Quadriga, which the Venetians took with them as a souvenir from Byzance during the fourth Crusade.

In more recent times, too, the Serenissima has been the target of a fair amount of criticism. The inflamed discussion about the "navi grandi", the cruise liners – which really doesn't affect anybody but the port, the shipping companies, city policy and the Venetians themselves – is keeping a number of busybodies occupied far beyond the city borders. Strangely, the fate of the Fondaco dei Tedeschi (the world's first trade mission, once founded by Germans) facing redesign plans, fades into the background. Probably because the forces involved like to make their moves in the shadows, and the fondaco was a less obvious provocation than a floating skyscraper.

Still, there is something positive about these shady sides too. Take the other meaning for the word "ombra" – which is a small glass of house wine, (until 2pm this is usually white wine, after that nearly always red wine). The ombra takes its name from the fact that the wine merchants on St Mark's Square, who were once allowed to display their "damigiane" (demijohns; in straw baskets containing wine) on long tables, would move with the shade of the Campanile to keep the wine cool and out of the sun. However, there is also a Venetian custom known as "giro de ombre", i.e. a kind of pub crawl, where more than just one ombra is taken, usually creating outright oblivion rather than the mere shadow of tipsiness.

Address Campanile (St Mark's Square), San Marco, 30124 Venice | Vaporetto fermata San Marco, line A, B, R, 2, 10 | Tip There aren't many places left in Venice still serving wine from the "damigiana" – in the Cantina do mori (San Polo 429) at the Rialto market this is mainly done for the ambience. On the Giudecca you can also find a wine shop selling "damigiane" – near the fermata Palanca (after getting off, continue on the left for some 100 metres, in the direction of Redentore).

82 The Pala d'Argento

An unknown hidden altarpiece

St Mark's has its "pala d'oro" (golden retable), the church of San Salvador has its "pala d'argento" (silver retable) – but most Venetians have never even heard of the latter. The reason being that you can only view it three times a year! At other times, the masterpiece of Venetian goldsmith art from the late 14th century remains hidden behind Tiziano's painting "Transfiguration of the Lord". Only on certain days of the year, the painting disappears into the bowels of the altar, moved by sophisticated counter-weights, allowing visitors to view the superb pala.

Just like the famous pala d'oro, the pala d'argento, too, was originally intended as a devotional altar, and is also only shown on special occasions. As the church of San Salvador is dedicated to Jesus Christ, the pala d'argento is shown to the faithful for the most important festivities connected with the son of God – to mark his birth, his resurrection (Easter Week), and the day of his transfiguration (6 August).

Following the Old Byzantine rite, the celebration of his transfiguration began as early as the 7th century on 6 August, the day when the first basilica was dedicated to the transfiguration on Mount Tabor. This event forms part of the Gospels. Following the miracle of the feeding of 5000, Jesus led the disciples Peter, James and John to the top of a high mountain. At that spot he was illuminated by a heavenly light, and a voice spoke to Peter: "This is my Son, follow him". The transfiguration is a symbolic anticipation of Christ's Resurrection. According to tradition, the place where this took place was Mount Tabor, located near Lake Gethsemane.

The pala d'argento consists of five elements placed on top of one another, with the main one showing the actual event of the transfiguration of the Lord.

Address Chiesa San Salvador, Campo San Salvador, San Marco 4827c, 30124 Venice |
Opening times The Pala may be visited three times a year: between 25 Dec and 1 Jan;
from Easter Sunday to the first Sunday after Easter; and between 6 and 13 Aug | **Vaporetto
fermata** Rialto, line A, 1, 2, night route N | Tip The frescoes in the sacristy of the church
of San Salvador are also well worth seeing. However, they may only be viewed by
appointment – best to enquire by email (sansalvador@inwind.it).

83 The Pink Pillars

So why the change of colour?

On the western facade of the Palazzo Ducale, two of the columns facing the Piazzetta, in the uppermost loggia as well as the railings, are pink, while all other columns and railings are white. This visual distinction was chosen deliberately, because during official ceremonies the space between the two columns was reserved for the Doge.

However, the two pillars had another far more sinister function too: death sentences were proclaimed between them and – if the condemned delinquent was a Patrician – also executed. All other criminals sentenced to death were led to the scaffold set up between the two columns at the Bacino di San Marco (see page 184) and executed there.

This custom is what the Venetian saying "guardate de'll entrecolumni" (avoid crossing columns) refers to, and a superstition developed out of this custom has remained relevant to this day; you'll hardly find a Venetian walking through these two columns – it could bring bad luck!

Here's one interesting detail: as soon as the condemned had been led onto the scaffold, they were able to determine the exact moment of their demise – for whom the bell tolls, Venetian-style. While the bell tower, itself, was not used for executions, it did serve torturing purposes. The condemned person was locked in what was known as a "cheba" (Venetian for cage), mounted half way up the clock tower and exposed to the elements.

The Bacino dei San Marco, too, was sometimes used for carrying out death sentences, with the condemned simply being drowned. In the Bacino Orseolo, too, right behind St Mark's Square, where gondolas and tourists vie for space, death sentences were also realized by drowning.

Address Doge's Palace, San Marco 1, 30124 Venice (the ninth and tenth column, counting from the Porta della Carta) | **Vaporetto fermata** San Marco, line A, B, R, 2, 10, night route N | **Tip** Can you see the two small lights on the southwestern side of the Doge's Palace? They are always burning, and their function is to remind us of one of the few judicial errors committed by the Serenissima: a certain, Piero Tasca, was unlucky enough to be wrongly charged with murder on circumstantial evidence, and under torture confessed to a crime he hadn't committed. He was condemned to death on 25 March 1507. The real culprit was only caught a good while later. The lights serve as a memorial and reminder for the judiciary not to carry out death sentences too swiftly – which led to many condemned criminals having to wait ten years or more for their execution.

84__ The Rangone
A remedy against syphilis

Above the entrance to the church of San Zulian, a sculpture shows the physician and scholar, Tommaso Giannotti (1493–1577), better known as T. Rangone, as he took on the name of his master, Count Guido Rangone.

The strange fact that the figure is holding a branch in his right hand is not entirely random, symbolising Rangone's discovery of a plant native to South America, which found use as a natural remedy against syphilis. In his left hand, Rangone is holding an open book with the inscription "HIQ" (hinc illincque), which can translate as either "from each side" or "on both sides". This is a reference to his opinion that you may know God both in the macrocosm and in the microcosm, both in Heaven, as on Earth. It is also no coincidence that the sculpture is shrouded in a talar, the symbol of infinite learnedness – Rangone was vain, and, well, he did put up the finance for the church facade.

However, Rangone's reputation was unfortunately impaired again and again by his annoying tendency towards self-promotion. His contributions to medicine are undisputed, and the fact that he restored the crumbling church of San Zulian has been much appreciated. Yet he was also a master at boasting; about his knowledge of astrology and linguistics, his skills as a doctor, and, last not least, his library, which he lauded as one of the seven wonders of the world. His true fame, however, is connected to his discovery of a remedy against syphilis – which was worth quite a bit in the hotbed of sin that was Venice!

Last but not least, based on the passage from the Bible Genesis 6.3, Rangone compiled a work entitled "How to Extend the Life of Humankind Beyond 120 Years". His basic recommendation was to lead a healthy modest life and to stringently curtail the use of medication.

THOMAS PHILOLOGVS RAV

Address Church of San Zulian, Campo San Zulian, San Marco, 30124 Venice | **Vaporetto** **fermata** Rialto, line A, 1, 2, night route N | **Tip** A popular location for today's self-promoters is the famous Harry's Bar (www.cipriani.com), where they not only mix a mean Bellini (white peach pulp with prosecco), but also where the popular "carpaccio" dish was invented and named after the renowned painter, Vittore Carpaccio, well-known for his palette of beefy reds. The original carpaccio only consisted of chilled raw beef, sliced very thinly with a knife and decorated with a light mayonnaise sauce "alla Kandinsky". Or maybe you prefer to do as Hemingway did and simply enjoy a glass of champagne.

85_ The Ridotti

The first state-run casino

Originally, "ridotti" were small rooms that the Venetians used as retreats to make secret contacts or to abandon themselves to unrestrained carnal pleasures. In use since the 13th century, these were later also used for casinos.

Before the advent of casinos, legal gambling only took place in the open air. Traditionally, the square between the column of the winged lion and the one dedicated to Saint Thedore, on the Piazzetta San Marco, was the chosen spot for this activity (see page 184). With gambling soon reaching all levels of society, the ridotti quickly achieved fame as being a particularly suitable spot for a quick game. In 1638, in order to better control gambling, which was getting out of hand, the Republic opened the first state-run casino in the rooms of the Palazzo Marco Dandolo, which would soon become world famous.

Gambling only took place during the Carnival season and was managed by impoverished noblemen, known as Barnabotti, in exchange for being allowed to live in houses allocated to them in San Barnaba. The rules were laid down by the government: only card games were allowed, the banker always had to be a Patrician, absolute silence had to be maintained during a game, and, apart from the croupiers, identified by their togas and curly wigs, all visitors had to wear a mask. The Venetians were fanatical gamblers, some betting everything on one card during the game of "Faraone" – and poof – gone was their Palazzo!

For instance on a single evening during the carnival of 1743, the Duchess of Modena lost a thousand zechines (about 3.5 kilograms of gold) to banker Gregorio Barbarigo. In 1774, the Great Council closed the casino down, to the great satisfaction of the moralists, who'd always objected – not for the gambling, but because the ridotti had remained what they'd always been – fornication venues.

Address Ridotto rooms in the Hotel Monaco e Grand Canal, Calle Vallaresso, San Marco 1332, 30124 Venice, www.hotelmonaco.it | **Opening times** Viewing of the rooms is only possible for hotel guests | **Vaporetto fermata** San Marco, line A, B, R, 2, 10, night route N | **Tip** In the past, the Palazzo Corner Contarini dei Cavalli used to house a famous casino; today it mainly consists of offices of municipal authorities. There is one room here, by the way, which is nearly entirely covered with Dutch tiles depicting animals, houses and mills – outside official hours, visits are permitted by request.

86__The Traghetto del Buso

Crossing over to the truck

Coming from San Marco, just before the stairs to the right and below the Ponte di Rialto (across from the Fondaco dei Tedeschi), you will find a remarkable place known as Traghetto del Buso (Ferry of the Hole). The Traghetto is a reminder of the location from which the gondolieri transported clients to the prostitutes (not the courtesans!) of San Polo. The Venetian word "buso" means hole and as slang refers to the female sexual organ. However, it also referred to a specific coin used to pay for the crossing, which had a hole in the centre.

In Venice, a distinction emerged early on between (low-level) whores and the (educated) courtesans, which is why 1535 saw the publication of the "Catalogo di tutte le principal et più honorate cortigiane di Venezia", with names, prices, qualities and the details of their procuresses. The highest level, and best paid women, were the "cortigiane oneste" (honest courtesans), who would usually have only one suitor or benefactor, were attractive and had a high level of education. The next category down were the less respected, "cortigiane da candela" or "cortigiane da lume", who practiced their profession in back rooms or brothels and were dependent on more than one suitor. "Putane", simply prostitutes, formed the lowest level.

While the courtesans – favoured by influential suitors – were able to walk the streets of the city in their finery unhindered, the whores had no rights and were only allowed to live in basic accommodations with sparse furniture. They also were not allowed to wear jewellery, go to church during Mass and religious feasts, give testimony at criminal trials, nor even take clients to court who refused to pay. They were also heavily disadvantaged in financial terms, compared to the courtesans; "price ratios" of 1:50 were not uncommon.

Address Right in front of the restaurant Al Buso, Fondamenta del Traghetto del Buso, San Marco 5338, 30124 Venice | **Vaporetto fermata** Rialto, line A, 1, 2, night route N | **Tip** The spaces between the windows on the facade of the former Fondaco dei Tedeschi used to be adorned with huge nudes, which have nearly all been lost. At least some remnants of these frescoes have been preserved, following elaborate restoration work, and are on view at the Galleria Franchetti in Ca' d'Oro. The Ponte di Rialto, too, was once decorated with obscene representations of the female sex – however, these provocative representations were already at the time retouched.

87__The Veneta

With sword and lions

One of the columns of the Doge's Palace features a tondo instead of the usual quatrefoil, with possibly the oldest still preserved representation of the Veneta – sitting on a throne, holding a sword and flanked by two lions.

According to legend, the origins of the city of Venice go back to the biblical people of the Venetkens, a subtribe of the Paphlagonians from Asia Minor. The Venetkens were a warrior people, with a thirst for knowledge. Their main deity was Reitia, the equivalent of Hera in the Greek pantheon. The Paphlagonians called the planet Venus, Reitia, meaning the "Honest, Just and Noble", later adding "Serenissima" (Most Serene). This referred to the ancient mother deity on the one hand, and to the autonomy of the city (long before the Roman era), on the other.

Veneto (Venetia) comes from the Latin, Uenus, meaning Venus, and is made from the Sumerian "W" for daughter and "anu" for sky; so Venus is the daughter of the sky. In ancient mythology, Venus was not only the goddess of the evening, promoting love and lust (these two areas seem to have turned themselves into the motto of this love-crazed city), she was also the goddess of the dawn, or aurora associated with war and conquest. This is quite fitting, as the Venetkens were, indeed, a warrior people. By day, Venus may be seen both in the east and in the west, which makes it an important symbol for both death and rebirth. The death mask the ancients laid on the faces of the dead picks up on this idea. In Venice this ritual has survived in Carnival, where the masks were often associated with melancholia (see page 84). With its "love and sword" symbolism, the tondo embodies Venice's connection with Venus, yet also the eventual transition to the lion as the symbol of the city and its patron saint, St Mark.

Address Doge's Palace, Piazzetta San Marco, San Marco 1, 30124 Venice on column no. 13 (counting from the Molo/waterbasin) of the west facade | **Vaporetto fermata** San Marco, line A, B, R, 2, 10 | **Tip** They say that the architect of the Santa Maria della Salute basilica was inspired by the temple of the Venus Physizoa, described in the novel "Hypnerotomachia Poiphili" (Poliphilo's Dream); the basilica, then, would represent the ring, uniting the veneration of the Virgin Mary with the old Venetian Venus deification.

88__ The Violinist

Vivaldi, celibacy and young ladies

Inside the little-known Museo della Musica, housed in the deconsecrated church of San Maurizio, the portrait of a violinist, partly hidden by old musical instruments, provides an opportunity to recall two interesting stories.

Thanks to official documentation, the life story of Antonio Vivaldi (1678–1741) has been passed down to us. We know that he was ordained as a priest in 1703, which, in principle, condemned him to a life of celibacy. That this wasn't taken terribly seriously in Venice was an open secret. However, surprisingly little is known about the actual relationship of Vivaldi with his young female pupils in the Pietà. His relationship, with a certain violinist named Anna, was particularly close and intimate – after all, Vivaldi wrote 30 violin concertos for this young lady, who would later become his "colleague".

Vivaldi was also said to have had an affair with singer, Anna Girò, who frequently collaborated with the composer, spending the last years of his life with him. However, despite recriminations that Vivaldi was breaking his celibacy with her – officially this lady was his housekeeper – his priesthood was never removed. The whole situation was all the more precarious because her sister, Paolina, was also living under the same roof; in which capacity is not known.

Venice has numerous stories about all these unusual relationships, and the conversation often oscillates between fact and fiction like gondolas on the waters of the canal.

Oscillating is also a word that could be applied to the musical taste of the Venetians, which explains why Vivaldi suddenly suffered the fate of no longer being considered modern. The Serenissima's appetite for ever-new "divertimenti" removed the artist's livelihood, forcing him to emigrate; Vivaldi died in Vienna and was buried there in a pauper's grave.

Address Museo della Musica in the Chiesa San Maurizio, Campiello Drio la Chiesa, San Marco 2603, 30124 Venice (the painting hangs at the back to the right, in the corner next to the former altar) | **Opening times** Daily 10am–7pm | **Vaporetto fermata** Giglio, Linie A, 1 | **Tip** Vivaldi's birth was registered in the church of San Giovanni Battista in Bragora, where he was also christened – he always called himself a son of the parrocchia. Opposite the church, the Antica Torrefazione Girani (www.caffeegirani.it) is one of the last coffee roasters in Venice.

89_Whimsical Columns

How throwing the dice became legal

The space between the two columns on the Piazzetta San Marco (the section between the Doge's Palace and the library) has an interesting connection with gambling.

The piazzetta is dominated by two monolithic columns; one is dedicated to the patron saint of Venice, Saint Mark (winged lion), the other to Theodorus (Todaro on the dragon), the patron saint of the first inhabitants of the Veneto. The piazzetta was used for receiving guests of state, executing the condemned – and for gambling: this was the first legalised place for the game of dice. Why gambling was allowed here and nowhere else, has to do with the columns: the two monoliths of red and grey granite come from the Orient and for a long time lay on the ground, as no one knew how the unwieldy round pillars could best be erected.

In 1172, engineer Nicola Starantonio Barattiero (who built the first Rialto bridge), raised the columns using a clever technical manoeuvre. As payment, the shrewd and enterprising Barattiero demanded permission to organise games of dice beneath the columns, despite, or, rather, because this game was banned. He duly received his obscure reward, opening Venice's first legal gambling den in the shadow of the twin pillars.

Aside from this location, gambling in Venice had a bad reputation and was conducted in more or less secret ridotti (see page 178). Still, gambling addiction managed to plunge countless noble and wealthy families into destitution. Turning vice into virtue, the Republic opened state-run casinos and employed the impoverished gambling-mad noblemen as croupiers – not entirely selflessly. As a result of these passionate gamblers, as well as through rules that definitely gave the advantage to the house, a large part of the earnings entered state coffers.

Address Monoliths on the Piazzetta San Marco, San Marco, 30124 Venice | Vaporetto fermata San Marco, line A, B, R, 2, 10, night route N | Tip The weathered fresco on the ceiling of the Sotoportego, where the Calle dei Fabbri crosses the Rio Terà de le Colonne, still shows a lantern, dice and the year 1691. While the fresco is definitely more recent, it does serve as a reminder of the first legal gamble.

90___24 Hours

Memories of an Italian clock

Most of the visitors strolling on the Piazza di Rialto today grant the large clock at the church tower of San Giacomo di Rialto only a fleeting glance. Yet both the building and the clock offer interesting details.

Following the Rialto fires of 1531 and 1601, the church was reconstructed and restored. Today's building, then, is a kind of modern copy, taking its architectural cue from the 1601 church – though, in fact, only reusing the pillars; the rich mosaics which used to adorn the vaults, for instance, have sadly been lost.

One of the truly remarkable features of this church is the steps, which were added when the original floor of San Giacomo was substantially raised to protect against flooding during the 17th-century reconstruction.

The large 15th century clock is a fine example of a real "Italian clock", with a 24-hour dial. After centuries of measuring time by sundials, at the end of the 13th century the first mechanical clocks appeared that could show the exact hour.

The day had 24 hours and started with sunrise, which is the reason why the face of the clock begins with 18 (rather than with 12 or 24 hours). At the end of the 14th century, most cities removed their sundials, as by then the bells of the church towers were marking the time.

However, it soon became clear that the number of rings was often confusing, leading to the system being simplified in the 15th century, with the bells no longer ringing 24 times, but only six times.

Under Napoleon's occupation, most of the Italian clocks disappeared and were replaced by the French clock, which was divided into 12 hours and began the day at midnight.

Address Clock at the tower of San Giacomo di Rialto, Ruga dei Oresti, San Polo 78c,
30125 Venice | Vaporetto fermata Rialto Mercato, line 1, night route N | Tip The famous
clock at the Torre dell'Orologio (clocktower) of San Marco is a relic of a Venetian clock,
with the Italian 24-hour dial.

91__ The Aretino Commemorative Plaque

An anticlerical and pornographic free spirit

On the facade of the Pescheria Nuova, you can make out a modern work by artist, Guerrino Lovato. It's a representation of Pietro Aretino, made of colourful glazed terracotta. Mounted in 2001, the commemorative plaque is a copy of a medallion made by sculptor, Alessandro Vittoria, produced at the time for the man of letters. A free spirit all his life, Aretino was born in 1492, the son of a shoemaker in Arezzo, but he denied his true origins, calling himself – not without self-mockery "the son of a courtesan and a king". From 1527 to 1556, he lived opposite the fish market on Canal Grande in Palazzo Bollani.

Aretino was not only feared as an arts critic, but also infamous for writings ridiculing the sacraments, mirroring his hostility towards the papacy. This anti-clerical stance made him flee to Venice, which at the time enjoyed a greater independence from the Pope. Venice, however, wasn't spared either, with Aretino openly claiming Venetians didn't know how to eat or drink.

Far better known than Aretino's criticism, are his "Sonetti lussuriosi", libertine works suffused with eroticism and obscenity. With illustrations by Giulio Romano and sold under Aretino's name, the Ex Libris sketch nothing but copulating couples, in various positions and in all sorts of locations, and also includes representations of the female sex – porn with a naturalistic exactitude.

Aretino revered a high-end courtesan named Angela Zaffa, who, according to him, was an absolute genius in the department of kissing, petting and intercourse. Now he wasn't one to keep her love artistry all to himself; one day he invited his closest friends, Tizian and Jacopo Sansovino, to partake, with the words: "I can offer pheasants and Zaffetta."

A PIETRO ARETINO 1492 1556

"LA VERITÀ È FIGLIA DEL TEMPO" DAGLI AMICI 2001

Address Pescheria Nuova, San Polo, 30125 Venice | **Vaporetto fermata** Rialto Mercato, line 1, night route N | **Tip** Aretino died in 1556 in Venice; just before his death, Pope Paul IV placed his works in the first compilation of banned books, the Index Librorum Prohibitorum. This makes it even more remarkable to have a relief of Aretino's head adorn the door to the sacristy in the St Mark's Basilica – a clear sign of Venice's stance towards Rome.

92__ The Bancogiro
Non solo Spritz

Campari soda is nice, but it's kind of "yesterday's news". Today, if you want to be with it, you have to drink Spritz. While Venice has long since emancipated itself from Austria, this doesn't apply to phonetics yet. The word spritz is short for G'spritzten, the wine and soda water drink common in the neighbouring country, which, together with a little elderflower syrup becomes a Kaiserspritzer (Emperor's spritz).

However, there are more words commonly used in Venice that go back to the Austrian occupiers. Just think of strudel and krapfen, which are clear Austrianisms, or schèi, a word for money, that derives from "schellini" (shillings). There's another curiosity visitors can witness during winter in Venice when the icy winds whistle through the narrow alleyways and the Serenissima completely hides its serene side. That's when loden wool wear comes into its own, with any Venetian worth their salt wearing this traditional Austrian-Alpine garb that you'll rarely see in the rest of Italy or on tourists.

But let's get back to spritz, which means going back to the Bancogiro, named for the first giro bank that was founded here. The Bancogiro is truly the best place to enjoy this drink, but only as "spritz al bitter" or "spritz alla venexina", made with Campari – not with the trendier Aperol or the far too adventurous Cynar. One permitted alternative, however, is Select, the Venetian version of Campari.

The best place for the drink is at the bar downstairs, where young and hip Venice meets. It is mixed from prosecco or Soave, Campari and soda water, served on the rocks and garnished with lemon peel and a green olive. A view of the canal is thrown in, the most stylish way to enjoy your spritz. Add a San Daniele ham, cured for two years, and you've found your new local.

Address Osteria Bancogiro, Campo San Giacometto, San Polo 122, 30125 Venice, www.osteriabancogiro.it | **Opening times** Tue–Sun 9am–midnight | **Vaporetto fermata** Rialto Mercato, line 1, night route N | **Tip** Above the entrance to the Palazzo Loredan a German-language inscription catches the eye: "K.K. STADT UND FESTUNGS COMMANDO", another reminder of the 19th-century Habsburgian occupation, when their military headquarters were established. By the way, over on the Giudecca, the "al Palanca" restaurant displays a panel showing all imaginable combinations for spritz.

93_ The Barbacan
A model for all of Venice

On the facade of a house at the end of the Riva del Vin, you can make out a beam hewn from Istrian rock displaying the inscription "Barbacan". The word presumably derives from the Arabic b-al-baqára, roughly translating as "Gate of the Cows" and was used as a kind of protective wall for the enclosure.

In the Middle Ages, the word "barbacan" was used for the reinforcement walls of military edifices and also stood for defensive walls equipped with embrasures. Last but not least, the counterfort walls connected to the reinforced paths within the walls were also called barbacan.

In Venice the word was initially used for wooden beams, later also for stone beams, which had the function of optimising the limited space in Venetian houses without narrowing or obstructing the streets and alleyways. For this purpose, the upper storeys were allowed to jut out beyond the ground floor, which increased the interior living space yet didn't impede the passage of pedestrians through the streets.

Barbacani can be found all over Venice, with a particularly well-preserved example in Calle del Paradiso, at the Campo Santa Maria Formosa.

Constantinople, too, had barbacani, very similar to their Venetian counterparts (the question of who copied the idea from whom remains unresolved).

Now, the barbacan mentioned at the beginning of this entry is very special, in so far as it served as a model for the construction of all other beams you see jutting out of the rows of houses in Venice.

All other barbacani had to follow this model, using the exact measurements decreed by the Venice city authorities.

Address Between the facades of the Riva del Vin, Calle della Madonna, San Polo 574, 30125 Venice | Vaporetto fermata San Silvestro, line 1 | **Tip** You can see what could happen when the strict construction regulations were not adhered to if you carry on a little in the direction of the market: Calle del Sansoni at the end of Calle Arco, number 965a, probably boasts the most lopsided house entrance in Venice.

94__ The Carampane

An exorbitant number of whores

In the past, a part of the island of Rialto was referred to as Carampane, because from the early 14th century onwards, mainly prostitutes lived here, offering their salacious trade (see page 208). Here they were allowed to display their wares in revealing clothing and by striking provocative poses, though after the third bell of San Marco they had to go back inside the house. And they were certainly not allowed to appear at church festivals.

However, over the course of time, prostitutes came to occupy ever-more space in the city, plying their trade where it happened to suit them. Seeing the reckless and shameless way they were drumming up customers, the city of Venice decided to ban these pleasure-providers and send them back to the house that they had inherited from a wealthy Venetian family, known as Rampani. The fact that they were allowed to use the former Palazzo Ca' Rampani led to the Venetian slang word for prostitutes, "Carampane".

In 1460, in order to curb the spread of prostitution, but also to prevent pimping and exploitation, various regulatory measures were laid down. This had little success, and so in 1539 the city fathers felt forced to simply ban all prostitutes who had been living in Venice for less than two years.

Yet, despite all efforts, the sex trade remained a booming business. On 21 February, 1543, the Senate decried the fact that there was an exorbitant number of whores in the city, claiming that one could find them in every lane, which meant that the Carampane concept of establishing a red-light district was deemed to have failed. Towards the end of the Venetian Republic, the term Carampane was only used for prostitutes, no longer for a particular neighbourhood. Also, 1776 saw the filling-in of the Rio de le Carampane, where today you'll find the Campiello Albrizzi. with its eponymous palazzo.

Address Campiello Albrizzi, San Polo, 30125 Venice | Vaporetto fermata San Silvestro, line 1 | Tip Not far from here, the Ca' Rampari is reached by heading straight from C. Albrizzi in the direction of the fish market, then taking a right at the first opportunity, then a left. The block of houses around Calle d'rio Rampani was the brothel. On some houses in the neighbourhood, behind the Rialto Market, you'll be able to spot various reliefs showing fruits of paradise, such as apples or peaches (see photograph). Remembering the history of the surroundings, it's probably not entirely accidental that the fruit always appear in pairs, referring, you can't help but wonder, to certain female curves?

95_ The Coopers

Wine barrels, wine merchants and a chapter house

In the area behind the Ponte di Rialto in the direction of the market, to the left, by the Campo Rialto Novo (New Rialto Square, as it is younger than the Campo di Rialto at San Giacometto) there was once a neighbourhood of various craftsmen's guilds – as evidenced by a few pillars dating from the 16th and 17th centuries that bear reliefs showing various crafts.

At house number 456, the wine merchants, in particular catch the eye; if you look more closely at the door, you'll notice that the lower part of the wall was broadened out into the shape of a barrel, in order to be able to roll the barrels in and out of the house more easily.

And the building with the number 551 displays a barrel – the symbol for the coopers' ("boteri") guild. To this day, the street named Calle dei Botteri, next to the fish market, serves as a reminder of the coopers who once lived here.

The barrels were not built here, but opposite the Jesuits' church, near the Fondamenta Nuove. In order to produce light and easy-to-handle barrels, the coopers would usually use high-quality oak wood, though chestnut or fir wood was also an option. Incidentally, the boteri were obligated to repair the barrels of the Doge's Palace for free.

In the nearby church of San Silvestro, you'll find the confraternity of wine merchants, who had their chapterhouse here (on the right-hand side of the church on the first floor), which may be visited – if a guide is present – during opening times. The chapterhouse was built by Chiona Lombardo between 1573 and 1581 – a few centuries earlier than the church itself. And the street name, Riva del Vin (Bank of Wine), is also a reminder of the once-mighty wine merchants guild.

Address Door cut out in the shape of a barrel, Calle de l'Arco, San Polo 456, 30125 Venice | **Vaporetto fermata** Rialto Mercato, line 1, night route N | **Tip** The house with the number 553 displays an image of a mulberry tree – the plant represented a silk manufacturers' residence here. Near the market, on a crossing pier at the intersection between Ruga dei Spezieri and the Ramo do Mori (house numbers 379 and 395) you can spot two reliefs with peaches – the symbol of the Persicata guild, which produced the peach jelly so popular in the Renaissance era.

96__ The Diving Suit
Underwater warfare à la Leonardo

Louis XII had barely been crowned King of France in 1498 when he claimed Milan, entering into a military alliance with Pope Alexander VI, as well as with the Venetian Republic in the spring of 1499.

The power of the Patrician family reigning in Milan collapsed; Ludovico Sforza had to flee, and his employee, Leonardo da Vinci, left Milan in December 1499, heading for Venice.

At the time, Venice was caught up in the second Venetian-Ottoman War (1499–1503), disputing territories in the Aegean, the Ionian Sea and the Adriatic. In August 1499, Venice lost the Battle of Lepanto – the first sea battle where ships were equipped with cannons. Eventually the city itself was besieged by Ottoman ships, as evidenced by contemporary paintings.

Leonardo offered the Lion City his services as an engineer, for the construction of war machinery, in particular. One of the marvels he presented was a diving suit with a breathing apparatus. Wearing this, soldiers were supposed to approach the Ottoman ships walking under water through the shallow lagoon and bore holes into the hull of the wooden Ottoman galleons to sink them. He also recommended the Venetians build war ships with double-walled hulls that would be protected from having holes bored into their own ships, as well as from being rammed by enemy vessels. The city fathers deemed both ideas to be pipe dreams, and the unemployed Leonardo left the city in 1500 for Mantua.

As was to become clear later, it was a fatal mistake on the part of Venice to let Leonardo go; modern reconstructions proved that the diving suit would have been completely functional. Having renounced this decisive military advantage, Venice had to concede defeat in 1503.

Address Museo Leonardo (next to the Chiesa San Rocco) Calle Tintoretto or Campo San Rocco, San Polo, 30125 Venice | **Opening times** Daily 9.30am–5.30pm | **Vaporetto fermata** San Tomà, line 1, 2, night route N | **Tip** Another great invention is the gelato for sale at "Grom un gelato come una volta" (www.grom.it), who run a branch here, just around the corner, at San Polo 3006. The sorbets made from real spring water, cane sugar and pure natural fruit extracts are also wonderfully refreshing.

97__The Mill

A games board or an esoteric symbol?

The Scuola Grande di San Rocco is famous for the Tintoretto masterpieces exhibited here. A small detail is often overlooked though: a stone standing next to the main entrance showing a mysterious game of Mills. Of course, it's possible that the pattern was simply carved into the stone to serve as a game board, however, we could also be looking at an "esoteric mill".

In many parts of the world the symbol, consisting of three concentric squares with four central lines in the inner square, is taken to be an esoteric symbol, representing the three phases of the spiritual path of the initiated. Three stages have to be passed before reaching the final goal: the corporal, the intellectual and the spiritual or divine.

Mills, or Nine Men's Morris was played in ancient Rome, Greece and Egypt. Supposedly, the board initially represented the three ring walls of Solomon's Temple; later it embodied the celestial Jerusalem with its twelve city gates (three on each side). The four cruciform lines connecting the three walls symbolise the paths used to spread the gospel. And the centre – which is known as the Fountain of Tradition – marks the point where the four symbolic rivers of paradise spring from.

In medieval Europe, many palaces and castles have three similarly laid-out ring walls, with special attention paid to the telluric forces (forces emanating from the earth) auguring a favourable place for spiritual contemplation.

The esoteric mill was also used as a sign denoting a holy place. This meant that people saw Venice as such a place – which, considering the secret messages that may be interpreted from the Tintoretto paintings kept in the Scuola (see page 210), is a distinct possibility.

Address Scuola Grande di San Rocco, Campo San Rocco, San Polo 3052, 30125 Venice (to the left next to the main entrance) | Opening times Daily 9.30am – 5.30pm | Vaporetto fermata San Tomà, line 1, 2, night route N | Tip On the first floor of the Fondaco dei Tedeschi you can find another Mills board, which, however, only served ludic purposes – now whether this Mills board will survive the reconstructions and restorations planned for the Fondaco is as uncertain as it is doubtful.

98___The Odd Inscription

A replacement for the former pillory

On Campo Sant'Agostin, a slate marker, with the mysterious inscription "LOC. COL. BAI. THE. MCCCX" is a reminder of the conspiracy instigated by Bajamonte Tiepolo on 14 June, 1310.

The grandson of Doge Lorenzo Tiepolo and great-grandson of Doge Jacopo Tiepolo, Tiepolo hatched his conspiracy with the aim of establishing a hereditary monarchy in Venice. The cause of the uprising was the "serrata" of 1297, limiting the right of access to the Great Council to a closed circle of noble families, with new additions only possible in exceptional cases. This developed into a power struggle between Venice's old ("Case vecchie") and new families ("Case nuove").

The leaders of the revolt were the aforementioned Bajamonte Tiepolo, his father-in-law, Marco Querini, and the Badoer family. Their opponent was Doge Pietro Gradenigo, from the apostolic Gradenigo family.

The conspirators were betrayed when the Doge became aware of the conspiracy early on, which explains how he was able to quash the revolt – which sparked off on 14 June 1310 – after just one day. Marco Querini was killed in the process (see page 168), and some of the Badoers arrested, condemned to death, and decapitated on 22 June, 1320. Bajamonte Tiepolo, himself, was able to negotiate very favourable conditions for his capitulation with the Great Council – he was exiled to Istria, which for him, a Croat, probably wasn't such a terrible punishment.

Tiepolo's house used to stand at the spot of this commemorative plaque. However, it was destroyed during the exile of its owner and a pillory was erected in its place. The pillory, though, has unfortunately disappeared (it is assumed to be in private hands on the banks of Lake Como). The slate marker is standing in place for the pillary, to commemorate the event.

LOC. COL.
BAL THE.
MO CX

Address Campo Sant'Agostin, San Polo 2304B, 30125 Venice | **Vaporetto fermata** San Stae, line A, 1, night route N | **Tip** There is another interesting plaque, in San Polo 2311 (Rio Terrà Secondo), reminding passers-by of Aldo Manuzio's printer's workshop. In 1501 Manuzio had the bright idea of setting the letters at an angle, to be able to increase the number of words, allowing for a smaller and cheaper printing format. This marked the birth of italics.

99_ The Papal Relief

The Pope and the Knights Templar

The Sotoportego de la Madonna hides many secrets, mainly to do with the fact that the building on the corner by Campo Sant'Aponal was once owned by Knights Templar, who were shrouded in secrecy. Turn around inside the Sotoportego and look up: you'll be able to make out some interesting representations mounted on the wall, that are a little hidden. One of them features the famous phrase, "Non nobis domine, non nobis, sed nomini tuo da gloriam nos perituri mortem salutamos" (Not to us, not to us, o Lord, but to thy name give glory; we who are vowed to death praise you). Looking more closely, you'll be able to make out a small figure of a Knight Templar hiding in a small niche. None of these representations go back to the Knights Templar (nothing having come down to us from their era), but they date from the Renaissance of the neo-Templar movement, which had the "Casa della Madonna dei Poveri Compagni d'armi di Cristo e del Tempio di re Salomone" built here.

In front of the small Templar statue, a wooden beam with an inscription and a small relief is a reminder of a legend. When Pope Alexander III came to Venice to make peace with Frederic Barbarossa, it was said that he refused to stay the night in the nearby former palazzo of the Patriarch out of fear of a plot on the part of the Emperor, and chose the street, instead. This legend has since been refuted. While it's probably true that the Pope didn't spend the night in the Patriarch's palazzo, he wouldn't have slept in the street, but would have been welcomed as a guest of the Knights Templar. After all, the Templars occasionally formed the Papal guard. Still the legend of the sleeping Pope has remained alive and if you say the Lord's Prayer and an Ave Maria at the small statue of the Pope to commemorate the event, you'll be forgiven for all your sins – now how does that sound?

Address Entrance from the Sotoportego de la Madonna, San Polo, 30125 Venice (at the corner between Calle de la Madonna and Calle del Perdon, to the left immediately beyond the entrance) | **Vaporetto fermata** San Silvestro, line 1 | **Tip** In the same Sotoportego you'll see a cross resembling the famous Maltese Cross of the Knights Templar – still, don't be tempted to connect this cross with the Templars, this here is a "Venetian cross".

100__ The Ponte delle Tette
Bare-breasted bait

Far more interesting than the less-than-mesmerizing Ponte delle Tette, is the story hiding behind this curious bridge's name – which, translated literally, means "Bridge of Tits". During the Serenissima's heyday, the part of town behind the Rialto bridge was considered a red-light district. According to a census completed in 1509, 11,164 prostitutes were offering their services in the city, practically the equivalent of a tenth of the population of the day. However, vice being what it is, it's always subject to strict stipulations on the part of the authorities (see page 196).

That applied to Venice too – even though the tax paid by the working girls provided the funds for the expansion of the Arsenal. One decree, however, was demanded by the prostitutes themselves: when, in the 16th century, there were far too many prostitutes in the city, their income sank dramatically.

Also, homosexuality was so widespread in Venice at the time, that these women of the night asked the Patriarch of the day, a certain Contarini, to take measures against it. Homosexuality represented a far bigger problem for them than inflation, making the men far less likely to need these female prostitutes for their sexual satisfaction.

As the Venetian government, too, preferred men to engage in the pleasures of the flesh with women rather than with other men, they ordered the prostitutes to show off their wares, with bare breasts or legs spread wide, to awaken tired male loins … a tantalising and arousing means of advertisement. The countless streetwalkers, with all their bared breasts and gathered-up skirts, must have presented an eccentric sight, indeed, of which today only the name of the bridge remains. Using naked skin to flog goods is still successful, however: "Sex sells!"

Address Ponte delle Tette, San Polo, 30125 Venice | Vaporetto fermata Rialto Mercato, line 1, night route N | Tip Alongside the Ponte delle Tette there's also a Fondamenta and a Calle delle Tette. And near the Ponte delle Tette you have the famous restaurant, Antice Carampane (www.anticecarampane.com), another indication of the extent of prostitution at the time.

101__Prophet Postel
Tintoretto's secret messages

In the Republic of Venice "Scuole" were confraternities: religious and charitable coorporations, crafts and guilds or associations of expats. While the "scuole piccole" were mainly craftsmen's corporations, the financial heavyweights "scuole grandi" were charitable organisations.

Now the Scuola Grande San Rocco shelters a few remarkable Tintoretto paintings; the artist is said to have used the esoteric doctrines of the French prophet, Postel. The paintings were commissioned by the confraternity, which saw Postel's teachings as a source of inspiration. The most important work in this context is "The Adoration of the Three Magi". This painting depicts a man in pilgrim garb with a surprising resemblance to the prophet Postel. According to the prophet's teachings, the painting should be interpreted in the following way: Venice is seen as the New Jerusalem, and the saints in the picture are invoking a second Messiah, who according to Postel, is a woman. This female Messiah supposedly completed the mission begun by Jesus – the Son of God having sacrificed his life for mankind to release them from their sins, while the new female Messiah would attain the same for women and unshackle them from the consequences of Eve's Fall. In this way, humankind was supposed to reconnect with its original purity, ending all religiously motivated wars, and the era of universal harmony could begin. For Postel, a certain Mother Giovanna, who worked in the Ospedaletto, embodied this female Messiah, turning Venice into a holy place (see page 202).

Apparently the church was not particularly interested in harmony, charging Postel with heresy. Arrested by the Venetian Inquisition, he was taken to Rome, declared of unsound mind and condemned to life-long incarceration.

Address Scuola Grande di San Rocco, Campo San Rocco, San Polo, 30125 Venice, www.scuolagrandedisanrocco.it | Opening times Daily 9.30am–5.30pm | Vaporetto fermata San Tomà, line 1, 2, night route N | Tip Hanging in the Sala Terrena, two of Tintoretto Mary paintings with trees also point to the coming of a female Messiah. Postel's teachings also mention a paradise on earth, with two kinds of trees, the "female" tree, unable to flower without the "male" tree of the same kind. This is a metaphor for the two-fold nature of the deity (female and male).

102 The Skeleton

Going to heaven with black magic?

When he took office, Doge Giovanni Pesaro (1589–1659) was eminently unlucky in his timing: he had contracted malaria and the Republic of Venice was standing at the brink of ruin, due to the Turkish Wars. Then Pesaro had to vacate Candia, Venice's base on Crete, was taken to court for strategic errors, and was humiliated for living with a cook, Dona Maria, though unmarried. However, Pesaro was a man of means and knew how to dazzle people; one of his show pieces was a bull-baiting event across the planks of a float on the Canal.

Pesaro earmarked 12,000 ducates in his will for the design of his tomb, in order to bridge the abyss between an illusion of greatness and the embarrassing reality. Unable to boast of any concrete achievements, he sought to represent his "merits", and thus attain immortality, with an overly elaborate wall tomb.

The grave invokes all-powerful evil in the shape of death holding the eulogy: the dark body tissue is dried-up, the leathery skin taut across the rib cage, the grotesque face set in an awful grin, the sunken eyes glinting maliciously from their deep cavities, the claw-like fingers clutching the marble eulogies. It's a ghostly vision, its message inscrutable. Did Pesaro really see himself as a hero who coming generations should remember, and who rose to heaven with the help of black magic? Or is he perhaps wishing all manners of evil onto the city that jeered him?

Pesaro had, in fact, only been elected Doge for pretending to plan the financing of the Venetian-Ottoman war with his private fortune – which, considering he was fully aware of his impending death from malaria – was no more than an illusion. He died after only one year in office. Pesaro wanted a triumphal arch to lead to his tomb and was one last time humiliated: his figure might stand above everything, however, amongst the dark forces he occupies a lost position, and not only visually.

Address Santa Maria Gloriosa dei Frari, Campo dei Frari, San Polo, 30125 Venice (the tomb is located to the left of the entrance, immediately beyond the Antonio Canova cenotaph) | Opening times Mon–Sat 9am–6pm, Sat from 1pm onwards | Vaporetto fermata San Tomà, line 1, 2, night route N | Tip Not far from the Frari church, at San Polo 2794, the Palazzo Centani is better known as the Casa Goldoni. Look closely, and you'll be able to make out a kind of spyhole typical for Venice: this kind of "viewing window" allowed one to watch what was going on in the streets, without being seen.

103_ The Two Lions

Power battles in the lagoon

Of the two remarkable stone lions standing at the Chiesa San Polo, one is fighting with a dragon-like creature, the other is holding a cut-off human head in its paws. The first lion is easily explained, symbolising Venice's fight against the troubles in the lagoon, which, after all, was thought to harbour a dragon (or crocodile; see page 144). Explaining the second one is not so easy, however, as there are two approaches, really, a historical one and another from the realm of legends.

According to mythology, the lion with the human head symbolises a certain Francesco Bussone, who fled to Venice in 1424, took over the Venetian troops here, and went on to win the Battle of Maclodio with them in 1427. However, his generosity with the prisoners aroused the suspicion of the Venetians. Following some military failures, he was ordered back to Venice in 1432, incarcerated for alleged treason and decapitated.

The historical variant seems more plausible. As the story goes, the head represents the Doge Marino Falier, who attempted a coup in 1355, to have himself proclaimed sovereign. The Great Council heard about the plan and had eleven conspirators arrested and hanged after a swift court martial. Falier, himself, was decapitated on 17 April, ironically on the same stairs (of the Scala del Piombo, razed in 1618), where he had been nominated Doge in September the year before.

The exact circumstances of the conspiracy are not known, however, as all court documents were destroyed in the course of a "condamnatio memoriae" (condemnation of the memory).

The idea behind both statues is that Venice (symbolised by the lions) has to fight for power with evil forces, both mystic (dragons) and real/human (decapitated head).

Address Chiesa di San Polo, Campo San Polo, San Polo 2011c, 30125 Venice (below the bell tower, exactly opposite today's entrance) | **Vaporetto fermata** San Tomà, line 1, 2, night route N | **Tip** In the gallery of Doge portraits kept in the "Sala del Maggior Consiglio" inside Palazzo Ducale, the spot intended for Marino Falier is occupied by a black banner with white lettering: "Hic est locus Marini Faletri decapitati pro criminibus" (This is the place of Marino Falier, who was decapitated for crimes). It was mounted by Tintoretto as a sign for the "condamnatio memoriae" (extinguishing the person's memory); the painting was already in place they say, but painted over by the banner.

104__ The Vulgar Relief
Obscene incidents within the financial administration

In contrast to what the name Palazzo dei Camerlenghi suggests, the palace initially didn't serve the city treasurers as a residence, but was the seat of the "Camerlenghi di comun", the financial administration of the Republic of Venice. Coming from San Marco, it's on the right-hand side of the Rialto bridge. Looking more closely, you'll be able to make out two fairly obscene reliefs that have in fact, a great deal to do with the history of the Rialto bridge: one shows a man with a disproportionately huge penis in the shape of a nail, the other shows a female figure with her intimate parts placed over a flame-spewing votive bowl. The two figures illustrated one and the same story surrounding the construction of the Rialto bridge.

After the wooden bridge had rotted or burned down several times, in 1507 the city administration decided to erect a stone bridge across the Canal. Decades of arguments about financing and design ensued, spurring the residents of San Polo, consisting of prostitutes, market traders, vendors and craftsmen, to make sardonic remarks.

The men would call out: "Sto ponte i lo finirà quando ch'ecl casso farà l'ongia" (if this bridge will ever be finished my penis will turn into a nail), and the women jeered an analogy: "Quando che i finisse el ponte, me ciaparà fogo la mona" (if the bridge should ever be completed my vagina will catch fire).

Both jibes were completely typical of the Venetian people of the time, forever incorporating obscenities into their jeering chants. Indeed, construction on the Rialto bridge started in 1588, and it was completed in 1591. Now the joke was on the local people, and the city administration used the two reliefs to show that the doubters were now due some "nails" or "flames".

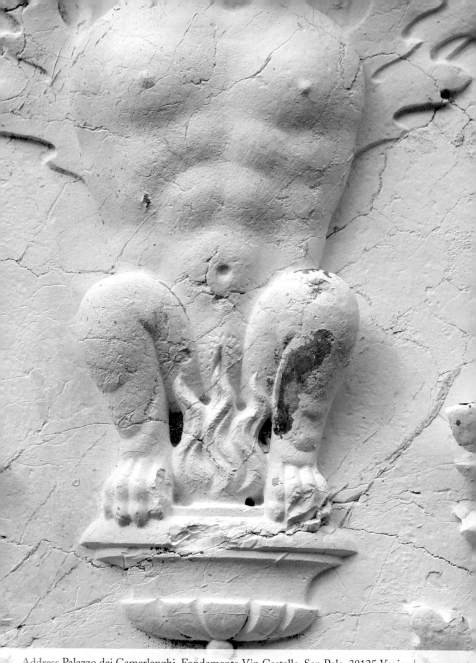

Address Palazzo dei Camerlenghi, Fondamenta Vin Castello, San Polo, 30125 Venice | Vaporetto fermata Rialto Mercato, line 1, night route N | Tip On the San Marco side of the Rialto bridge, looking towards San Polo, on the right, you'll come across the Restaurant al Buso, going back to the former Traghetto del buso (see page 180), and to the left, a little below the bridge, the Bar Aperol, famous for its great range of tramezzini.

105__ The White Masque

The legend of the honourable lady

Many rumours surround the mysterious white head casting its mystical gaze down onto the viewer from a plain brick wall. To this day, it's not been established whether this high relief is the mask of a woman or a man, giving rise to plenty of different legends.

Possibly the most interesting story is the one about a certain Santina, who was the beautiful and extremely attractive wife of a local sword manufacturer.

A young aristocrat named Marchetto Rizzo is said to have fallen head over heels in love with the charming lady and ordered a dagger from Santina's husband. Under the pretence of checking how work on his dagger was progressing, he visited the workshop on a daily basis, in order to be close to his planned victim. Shortly before the weapon was finished, Santina happened to be on her own in the workshop, which spurned the lovesick young man to rape the object of his passion. Unable to live with the humiliation, Santina took her own life with the commissioned sword, to save her honour.

A second story also tells of Santina and her young tormentor, yet in a much less violent form. A certain Zuane, a friend of Santina's weapon-making husband, is said to have preempted and foiled the aristocrat's plans. Even though he didn't kill the rapist during the fist fight, as far as it's known, Santina's saviour was banned from the city on 14 October, 1490, for six months.

Venice wouldn't be Venice if there wasn't a saucy addition to this story, as well. So an old gondoliere offered up the following version: in Venetian, the high relief is known as the "Honourable Lady", said to be one of the "honest courtesans" (see page 180), who applied very reasonable (i.e. "honourable") rates for her services.

Address Calle Forner S. Elena, San Polo 2935, 30125 Venice | Vaporetto fermata San Tomà, line 1, 2, night route N | Tip Walking from the Fondamenta della Dona Onesta across the Ponte della Dona Onesta, on the left hand side you'll find the venerable Trattoria Dona Onesta (www.donaonesta.com), which has been here since 1735.

106__ The Altane

"Forest" towers for women

The wooden "hunting" towers above the rooftops of Venice are not status symbols of nouveau-riche families treating themselves to a chic roof terrace, but have been a part of the cityscape – as evidenced by old documents – since the 13th century.

They were originally constructed in the same way as the hunting towers in the wooded foothills of the Alps, with a square wooden floor sitting directly atop the roof beams, on wood and brick supports, surrounded by a railing. Their initial function in the city was as an opportunity to breathe some "fresh air", but they were also handy for spotting enemy ships, as the views from these ranged across the entire lagoon way out to the open sea, and, on to the other side, far into Terraferma.

Over the course of time, the raised wooden platforms changed from being guard towers into more residential amenities, which were mostly enjoyed by women – a rendezvous on the altana (from the Latin "altus" = high) was a rare and accordingly sought-after adventure for the male world; even if the invite was issued by an honest working girl, this was something special, indeed.

Over the course of their changing identity, the altane were equipped with pergolas, sun sails, railings to beat carpets on, planters, seating and everything else you need on a veranda.

What has remained is that the altane are still used – mostly by women, not only to simply enjoy some fresh air and to spend leisure time, but also to watch what is going on in the city without being seen.

At Augusto Capovilla's workshop this kind of altane are still exclusively produced by hand, and if you keep quiet you might be allowed to watch the masters at work.

Address Augusto Capovilla sas (altane carpenter), Calle delle Oche, Santa Croce 853, 30135 Venice | **Opening times** As this is a traditional bottega (workshop), visiting is only possible by prior arrangement. | **Vaporetto fermata** Riva di Biaso, line 1, 5.1/5.2, night route N | **Tip** While most altane are made of wood, a few were made of stone – one of them, for instance, is to be found at the Palazzo Contarini, right next to the fine arts academy.

107__ The Ancient Column

What can this relic tell us?

The only thing still standing at the site of the former church of Santa Croce and its monastery is an ancient column which is set, more or less hidden, into a corner of the wall. Now the question is why did this slightly inconspicuous column remain upright? This issue has kept historians fairly busy, with three stories of particular interest.

One group of scientists assumes that the place where the column stands is exactly the spot where criminals condemned to death had their hands hacked off – in those days it was fairly customary to torture condemned delinquents who were guilty of particularly heinous crimes before the death penalty was carried out. First they would have their hands hacked off, then they would be beaten unconscious, before finally being beheaded. The body was usually burnt; the decapitated heads hung up as a deterrent.

Looking at the column a bit more closely, you may be inclined to agree more with a different story, one that focusses less on the column itself, and more on the far older capital.

The front shows stylized letters, when deciphered yield the following: "TIKHI".

These letters form the name of a town called Tikhil in southwestern Russia, which, for one thing, has a long connection with the Armenian church (still present in Venice), and for another, is said to be where the first Veneti came from – making it the true origin of the Venetians.

There is also a symbolic explanation for these signs. You could interpret the sign as an "H", too, the symbol of the esoteric teachings of Hermetism – in this reading, this double crossing of loops could also be the hermetic symbol of the Resurrection.

Address Fondamenta del Monastero, Santa Croce, 30135 Venice (on the corner of the Fondamenta di Santa Croce at the foot of the Santa Croce bridge, on the Canal Grande between the Papadopoli Gardens and the Rio dei Tolentini) | Vaporetto fermata Piazzale Roma, line 1, 2, 3; 4.1/4.2, 5.1/5.2, 6, night route N | Tip Not far from here the church of San Simeone Piccolo has the lowest church tower in all of Venice – it's only three metres high.

108__The Bomb

A reminder of Radetzky

The facade next to the entrance of the Chiesa San Nicola da To-
lentino (called I Tolentini) contains an Austrian bomb dating back to
1848. This is a reminder of the following story: on 21 December
1847, in the middle of the Risorgimento (see page 108), the lawyer,
Daniele Manin, handed the government a petition with suggestions
for reforming the constitution, for which the authors were arrested
on 18 January 1848, yet released again as early as 17 March. While
Lombardy was proclaiming their independence from Austria, join-
ing the newly founded kingdom, Manin, on 23 March 1848, proclaimed an independent Republic of Venice.

When on 5 July, 1848, the Venetians joined the young kingdom,
Daniele Manin had already stepped down two days earlier – claiming he couldn't serve as a subject to a king. On 25 July, the Piemon-
tese were defeated in the battle of Custozza, and recalled their fleet
from Venice. Faced with the now acute threat from the Austrians,
victorious at Custozza, Manin was proclaimed dictator and by the
end of the year the Austrian troops had conquered the entire Veneto.

On 4 May 1849, the Austrians first attacked the fortification of
the Marghera (near Mestre), taking it on the 26th. The Venetian revolutionary troops faced the Austrians on the Ponte della Libertà,
which connected the mainland with Venice, refusing a capitulation
demanded by General Radetzky. Venice was subsequently bombard-
ed for over 24 days, with more than 30,000 bombs, Radetzky being
of the opinion that Venice had to be completely sunk to break its resistance.

On 22 August 1849, the city, additionally weakened by a cholera
epidemic, had to surrender. On 27 August, the Austrian troops marched
in and went on to rule until 1866.

Address Chiesa San Nicola da Tolentino, Campo dei Tolentini, Santa Crocre 265, 30135 Venice | **Vaporetto fermata** Piazzale Roma, line 1, 2, 3; 4.1/4.2, 5.1/5.2, 6, night route N | **Tip** The interior of the church is also worth seeing; the fresco on the ceiling suggests a dome – even though the church has no dome but a flat roof. Another point of interest is the fact that today's Austrian consulate is located directly opposite the church – with a view of the bomb once sent by the Austrians! By the way: the small Barcareto da Lele in front of the church, on the right-hand side corner, offers up fine panini with simple house wines.

109___ The Eliminated Lion

Getting rid of an unloved icon

The city has its fair share of destroyed and damaged lions, in line with what used to happen to the heads of the Pharaohs in Egypt. The republic of the lion's emblem was not always loved, or was sometimes removed by foreign powers as proof of their triumph.

One place you can find the remains of former lions, for instance, is to the left below the Bridge of Signs on the wall of the lead chambers, on the wall of the Arsenal facing the lagoon, or on various building walls.

While the ones on public buildings were taken off by foreign occupiers, the ones on the walls of houses were removed by the Venetians themselves – and, once again, this has to do with the Bajamonte Tiepolo conspiracy (see page 204).

The history books tell us that following the 1297 serrata, only the established families of Venice, or "case vecchie", were allowed to elect the Doge or be elected Doge. Families who were given this right were listed in the Libro d'Oro, de facto excluding all other Patrician families, the nouveau-riche ("case nuove"), in particular. There was subsequent domestic unrest in the serrata's wake, not instigated by those excluded, but by the aristocrats who felt they'd been overlooked at the last Doge election. The foreign affairs failures of the Doge Pietro Gardenigo, as well as his anti-Papal policies and nepotism, increased the discontent, which was to culminate in the Tiepolo conspiracy.

But back to the lions: the walls of houses belonging to the families who had taken part in the said revolt were deliberately "adorned" with a St Mark's Lion. And, of course, the rebellious home owners would remove these unloved signs, symbolising those in power, as soon as possible. And where they didn't completely succeed in doing so, you'll find the preserved relics of knocked-down lions.

Address Ca' Zane, Campo Santa Maria Mater Domini, Santa Croce 2120 und 2121,
30135 Venice | Vaporetto fermata San Stae, line A, 1, night route N | Tip Vestiges of
other lions that have been destroyed can be spotted at the house of the conspirators' family,
Querini, in Calle delle Rasse or on the Ca' Loredan on San Canciano or on Ca' Corner at
the Santa Fosca bridge. Napoleon, too, had the signs of the Lion City in prominent places
taken down, for instance, at the lead chambers (below the Bridge of Sighs) or at the
Arsenal (rear entrance to the lagoon).

110_ The Palazzo Tron
Cantankerous ladies

At the high point of the Doges' political and financial power, Andrea Tron was the incumbent of the Doge's Palace. A remarkable man, this enlightened conservative was what today would be called a political realist. As an older man, he fell in love with Caterina Dolfin, the daughter of a Patrician dynasty that had fallen on hard times, and married her against the will of his brothers. Full of life, Caterina Dolfin liked to surround herself with literary folk and journalists, becoming their patron and fiery lover too.

Andrea's brother, Francesco Tron, went on to marry a woman 34 years his junior. 17-year old Cecilia Zen was his bid to maintain the dynasty, the marriages of his brothers having remained childless. Cecilia Tron must have been a real beauty; with considerable sexual charm, a good level of education and the ability to ride and fence like any man.

When Cecilia Tron returned to Venice, following the death of her husband, she became engaged in a rivalry with her much older sister-in-law Caterina, whom she tried to trump, using all available feminine wiles. She certainly managed this in the scandal department, showing up uninvited at official events dressed up in men's clothes, or wearing evening gowns that displayed her bare stunning breasts to best advantage. As the main heir of the Tron fortune, she moved into the Palazzo, forcing out her unloved sister-in-law, Caterina.

All her life Cecilia was to remain a femme fatale, who knew how to use her attributes, sometimes with negative consequences. For instance, her French-friendly stance during the French occupation brought her repeated house arrest under the Austrian rule that followed. Still, her amorous adventures and apparently extremely shapely breasts have made her the talk of Venetian society – to this day.

Address Palazzo Tron, Calle del Forno, Santa Croce, 30135 Venice | **Vaporetto fermata** San Stae, line A, 1, night route N | **Tip** A little further on in the direction of Rialto, from the Canal side you'll see a fine garden. This is where the Palazzo Contarini used to stand before it was destroyed in a fire in the mid-19th century and was completely torn down, rather than restored.

111___St John the Decapitated
A stew with human flesh

The Venetian name for the church of San Zan Degolà translates into Italian as San Giovanni Decollato, meaning "the Decapitated". This name for John the Baptist goes back to the famous story of Salomé, who demanded the head of John the Baptist from Herodes, for her mother, Herodias. John had reproached Herodes for having married Herodias (his sister-in-law).

The high relief in the church represents John the Baptist and the residents of this neighbourhood tell their children a macabre story to go with it: the relief is supposed to show a certain 16th-century butcher and innkeeper named Biasio Cargnico, who was known all over town for his fabulously tender sausages and a wonderful "squazzetto", or hearty meat stew. Business was booming, and his delicacies attracted plenty of customers. Until one day a worker discovered a fingertip with a tiny fingernail in his squazzetto!

Suddenly people realised that, for a while now, small children had been disappearing in this part of the city. The authorities were immediately alerted and Biasio publicly indicted. During his torture, the "luganegher" (sausage maker) confessed to his devilish acts – however, it couldn't be ascertained how long Biasio had been cooking this horrific recipe.

He was judged and had his hands hacked off in front of his shop, before being tied to the tail of his own horse and dragged to the two monoliths on the Piazzetta San Marco (see page 186), where he was decapitated. Afterwards he was quartered and exhibited in public. His residence, sausage factory and inn were burned to the ground and completely razed.

This history is no mere legend, by the way, but officially recorded in the Registri dei Giustiziati, the Venetian lists of the executed.

Address San Zan Degolà church, Campo San Zan Degolà, Santa Croce, 30135 Venice | **Vaporetto fermata** Riva di Biasio, line 1, 5.1/5.2, night route N | **Tip** Despite – or maybe because of – the gruesomeness of this story, both the river banks (Riva di Biasio) as well as the local Vaporetto stop were named after this Biasio. So, while his house and shop were razed, his name has remained – quite obviously that wasn't quite as easy to erase!

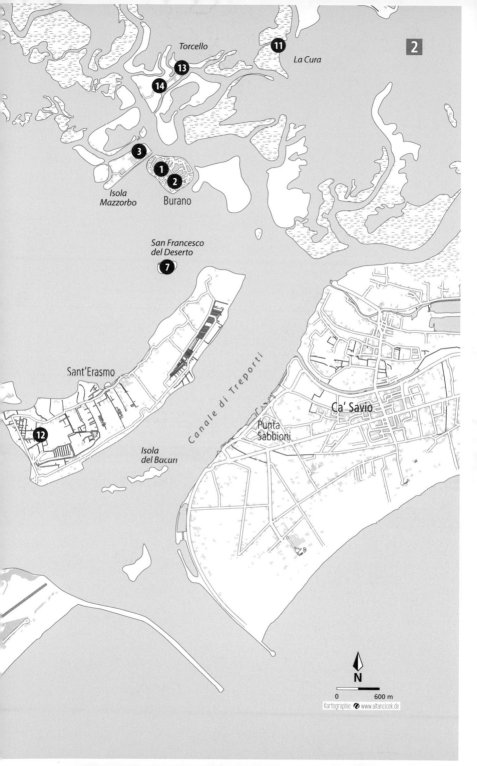

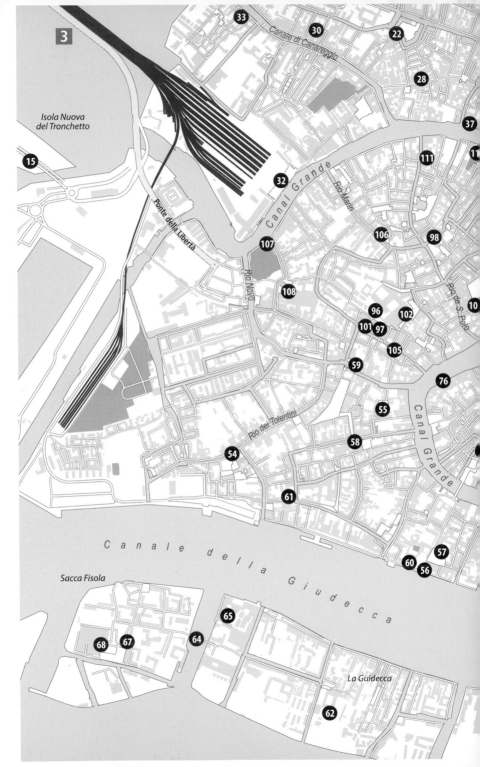

Lucia Jay von Seldeneck,
Carolin Huder, Verena Eidel
**111 PLACES IN BERLIN
THAT YOU SHOULDN'T MISS**
ISBN 978-3-95451-208-9

Rüdiger Liedtke
**111 PLACES IN MUNICH
THAT YOU SHOULDN'T MISS**
ISBN 978-3-95451-222-5

Rike Wolf
**111 PLACES IN HAMBURG
THAT YOU SHOULDN'T MISS**
ISBN 978-3-95451-234-8

Paul Kohl
**111 PLACES IN BERLIN
ON THE TRAIL OF THE NAZIS**
ISBN 978-3-95451-323-9

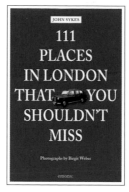

John Sykes
**111 PLACES IN LONDON
THAT YOU SHOULDN'T MISS**
ISBN 978-3-95451-346-8

Dirk Engelhardt
**111 PLACES IN BARCELONA
THAT YOU MUST NOT MISS**
ISBN 978-3-95451-353-6

Peter Eickhoff
**111 PLACES IN VIENNA
THAT YOU SHOULDN'T MISS**
ISBN 978-3-95451-206-5

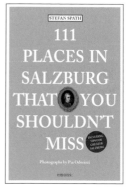

Stefan Spath
**111 PLACES IN SALZBURG
THAT YOU SHOULDN'T MISS**
ISBN 978-3-95451-230-0

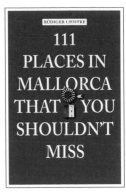

Rüdiger Liedtke
111 PLACES ON MALLORCA
THAT YOU SHOULDN'T MISS
ISBN 978-3-95451-281-2

Marcus X. Schmid
111 PLACES IN ISTANBUL
THAT YOU MUST NOT MISS
ISBN 978-3-95451-423-6

Ralf Nestmeyer
111 PLACES IN PROVENCE
THAT YOU MUST NOT MISS
ISBN 978-3-95451-422-9

Christiane Bröcker,
Babette Schröder
111 PLACES IN STOCKHOLM
THAT YOU MUST NOT MISS
ISBN 978-3-95451-459-5

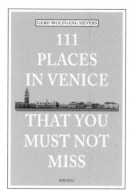

Gerd Wolfgang Sievers
**111 PLACES IN VENICE
THAT YOU MUST NOT MISS**
ISBN 978-3-95451-460-1

Annett Klingner
**111 PLACES IN ROME
THAT YOU MUST NOT MISS**
ISBN 978-3-95451-386-4

Susan Lusk, Mark Gabor
**111 SHOPS IN NEW YORK
THAT YOU MUST NOT MISS**
ISBN 978-3-95451-351-2

Kirstin von Glasow
**111 SHOPS IN LONDON
THAT YOU MUST NOT MISS**
ISBN 978-3-95451-341-3

The Author

Already at the age of five, **Gerd Wolfgang Sievers** was far happier at the stove than on the football pitch. Following a degree in journalism and communications, he passed his final examination to become a certified chef. Since then, Gerd Wolfgang Sievers has been writing culinary and gastro-philosophical columns in various specialist magazines and newspapers. To date, he has published twenty-five German-language books, amongst them various publications on Venice, where he lived for years. Today he works in Vienna and divides the rest of his time between the Burgenland in eastern Austria and the Friuli region in Italy.